The Indiana
Book of Trivia

The Indiana
Book of Trivia

Fred D. Cavinder

Indiana Historical Society Press
Indianapolis 2007

Printed in the United States of America

This book is a publication of the
Indiana Historical Society Press
450 West Ohio Street
Indianapolis, Indiana 46202-3269 USA
www.indianahistory.org

Telephone orders 1-800-447-1830
Fax orders 317-234-0562
Online orders @ shop.indianahistory.org

The paper in this publication meets the minimum requirements of American National Standard for Information Sciences—Permanence of Paper for Printed Library Materials, ANSI Z39.48-1984. ∞

Library of Congress Cataloging-in-Publication Data

Cavinder, Fred D., 1931–
  The Indiana book of trivia / Fred D. Cavinder.
    p. cm.
  Includes index.
  ISBN-13: 978-0-87195-252-3 (alk. paper)
    1. Indiana—History—Miscellanea. 2. Indiana—Biography. I. Title.

F526.5.C 368 2007
972.2—dc22

                                                            2006049611

Contents

Introduction

There once was a tongue-in-cheek, often-used reaction to the news that one's enemy is suffering from some malady. "Nothing trivial, I hope," was the reply used to show an insincere sense of concern.

In fact, triviality is as serious as anything in our culture short of something life-threatening or some event that is a hazard for our credit cards. When you think about it, the trivial has been the heart of some of our fondest pastimes and entertainments. At least as early as *The 64,000 Question* (before its revelation of fraudulence), the affection for trivia has been anything but trivial, right on down through the engrossing game Trivial Pursuit, and on to the millennium craze, *Who Wants to Be a Millionaire?*

Everyone wants to be a millionaire, of course, which is why it was so named to lure viewers. And trivia, when you investigate it, is a way to millions on that show. Yet, the accumulation of trivial data is not exactly a recognized talent. Let's say, for example, that Benjamin Franklin was the only person who signed both the Declaration of Independence and the U.S. Constitution. Interesting, but not something on which a value can be easily placed. It's not the sort of thing that works easily into casual conversation.

Some years ago a friend compiled some items that could be worked into conversations either when an embarrassing lull occurs or when you want such a pause to occur. Trivia can be the answer in either case. One of his suggestions was, "Did you know there are more than fifty active volcanoes in the world today?" I don't vouch for the number. Maybe it's thirty-nine. That's not the sort of trivia I admire. But it does raise a point: trivia has its practical uses.

While not attracted to volcanoes, I am more likely to pop out a bit of Indiana trivia, not so much when the conversation lags as when a hidden Hoosier opportunity occurs. Should someone mention the actor Clifton Webb (when *Cheaper by the Dozen* appears as a classic on television, as it sometimes does), I am likely to remark, "He was a Hoosier, you know." Usually, unless the audience includes some of my fellow fugitives from the newspaper business, only a few people know Webb's origins. Or care. But it is an interesting piece of trivia, considering that Webb portrayed characters far too acerbic, urbane, and disdainful to be logically considered a product of Indianapolis, as he was.

Newspaper people, in Indiana at least, usually are well versed in the Hoosier connections that have gained recognition elsewhere in the world. It's probably part of an Indiana bias that "once a Hoosier, always a Hoosier." All that aside, there is a gold mine of Indiana trivia out there, much of it surefire for wedging into conversational breaks.

This, then, is a bow to such mind-cluttering material, lying idle for the most part until a timely quiz show comes along. However, the attempt has been, considering there are many other books of trivia and a few devoted to Indiana, to present the really trivial trivia. First of all, there is little need to repeat what already is reasonably common knowledge, and second, a lot of Hoosier trivia that is not historically significant can stop conversations cold, even if you don't wish a lull to occur.

There seems little purpose in revealing that Cole Porter was from Indiana, that Hoosier Don Larsen pitched the only perfect game in World Series history, or that the Wonder Five of basketball came from Franklin. He is, he did, and they are, and many know it.

There is meatier material, odder, if less historic. For example, in 1912 J. Garland Stahl of Elkhart played in the second game of the World Series, the only series game to end in a tie. Stahl may not be important, Hoosier though he is, but it has a double trivial whammy because of the odd World Series game. Did you know the attendance record for an Al Jolson performance was set in Indianapolis? Don't snicker too loud. We are reaching a time when the name Al Jolson is itself a trivial fact that could pop up on quiz shows.

Besides, not all trivia is bursting with relevance or usefulness. A lot of it is just plain fun. One goal of this listing is to produce some entertainment. We're not doing *War and Peace* here, just a pleasant diversion. Hopefully a minority of the entries will be boring. And we hope very few of them seem so well known they don't rate inclusion here.

Above all, may some of them produce a pursed lip or a faint smile. There will be a few readers, no doubt, who will consider the entire enterprise a waste of paper. These few could perhaps say, "Reading this drivel made me sick." To which a logical reply might be, "Nothing trivial, I hope."

Agriculture

Beverly Shores in Porter County occupies the once marshy lands where cranberries were grown from the early 1800s to the early 1900s.

It is said that although Abraham Lincoln's family owned 160 acres in Indiana, only 18 acres were tillable.

The first corn-growing contest in Indiana was in 1913 in Randolph County, sponsored by Goodrich Bank at Winchester. Competitors numbered thirty-four, and the winner was James M. Garringer of Fairview, who won $50 of the $150 in prize money. The rules called for contestants to submit the best corn harvested from a five-acre plot.

Leonard B. Clore, Johnson County Corn King shortly after the turn of the twentieth century, won these prizes, among others, at corn shows: a 160-acre Texas farm, a piano, a stove, a watch, a clock, a mandolin, a lawn swing, and farm implements.

Solon Robinson, whose support of settlers in Lake County led to the founding of Crown Point, became a nationally known speaker, promoting improved agricultural conditions. In 1853 he became agricultural editor of the *New York Tribune*.

International Corn King titles have been bestowed over the years on fourteen Shelby County farmers, if not a record, surely an outstanding average.

When the Potato Museum opened in Washington, D.C., in 1985, artifacts included an Earthway Spada Potato Planter made in Bristol in Elkhart County. It was a device for sowing seed potatoes in a furrow. It had not been manufactured for more than a decade.

Marvin Johnson of Carthage won the first mechanical corn-picking contest in Indiana, harvesting 2,827 pounds of corn in about eight minutes at Rushville on October 13, 1951. He beat thirty-three contestants before a crowd of about thirty thousand and won one hundred dollars, a living room suite, a trophy, and a trip to the nationals in Benton County, Iowa, two weeks later.

The longest continuing auction of farm equipment is at the Stilesville farm implement auction west of Indianapolis, which has sold gear, usually by consignment, for more than seventy-five years.

Arts and Entertainment

Famed Indiana composer Cole Porter was left-handed. He wrote his first operetta, *The Song of the Birds*, when he was ten years old. Although crippled in 1937 in a horseback riding accident, Porter continued to compose until 1958 when amputation of his right leg and other health problems forced him to retire. He died six years later in California. During a period when he had to wear casts on his legs, he dubbed the casts Geraldine and Josephine.

Cole Porter was born in this house in Peru, Indiana.

Hoosier songwriter Cole Porter, a bon vivant, was one of the first to drive a speed-boat down the Grand Canal in Venice. In Paris, Porter's luxurious home at 13 Rue de Monsieur had one room that featured platinum wallpaper. His lavish lifestyle included many parties where the main requisite was that they not be dull; he once eliminated a guest from future soirees when it was found that the guest couldn't converse in French and, worst of all, wore brown shoes.

When Cole Porter lived in the prestigious Waldorf Towers in New York (1939–64), the Waldorf Astoria was so pleased to have him in residence there that it purchased a Louis XVI fruitwood grand piano by Steinway and gave it to Porter in 1945. The hotel obtained the piano after Porter's death, and the piano was made part of a lobby bar called Peacock Alley.

Among the forgotten Hoosier composers is Clarence Stout of Vincennes. Stout, descendant of Elihu Stout, founder of Indiana's first newspaper, never left Vincennes despite writing numerous published songs and staging productions in Vincennes using local talent. His first major hit was "O Death Where Is Thy Sting," performed in the 1919 Ziegfield Follics and recorded for Columbia Records by the noted black entertainer Bert Williams.

Noted Hoosier painter Otto Starke was first apprenticed as a wood-carver in the family furniture company. He turned to oils when he fell while driving the cows home and suffered an ankle injury that prevented him from being able to stand and carve.

Bohumir Kryl, a Bohemian who was an assistant sculpture to Rudolph Schwartz on the Soldiers and Sailors Monument in downtown Indianapolis, turned to the cornet after hearing Thomas Waldron, born in Lebanon, Indiana, play the instrument at the old English Theater on Monument Circle. Kryl became a world-renowned cornet player with the John Philip Sousa band.

James Forman "Tod" Sloan, who became a famous jockey in England and the inspiration for George M. Cohan's song "Yankee Doodle Boy," was born near Kokomo in 1874. Sloan also was a crack billiards player and an expert shot. He is credited with bringing the game of bridge to the United States from England and teaching it to such persons as baseball manager John J. McGraw in a billiards room on New York's Broadway.

The Indiana Dunes were a favorite site for movie makers in the early 1900s, including a 1910 film by a Chicago company, *Conquest of Mexico* in 1912, and *The Plum Tree* in 1914, starring Francis X. Bushman.

Fred Jewell of Worthington wrote more than two hundred musical numbers for bands and was considered by many to be as good as his contemporary, march king John Philip Sousa. Jewell played and directed circus bands, including those of the Ringling Brothers Circus and Barnum and Bailey Circus.

"Back Home Again in Indiana," which is really titled "Indiana," was the first song hit written by James F. Hanley of Rensselaer. The song sold two million copies before Hanley died in 1942 at the age of forty-nine. During his adulthood he was so shy that few photographs were taken of him, and he had friends introduce him as a businessman to avoid possible adulation for his music. Hanley wrote many popular tunes, including "Second Hand Rose," his second big hit, and "Zing! Went the Strings of My Heart." The words to "Indiana" were written by Ballard MacDonald.

James H. "Babe" Pierce, native of Freedom in Owen County, not only played Tarzan in the movies, he also married Joan Burroughs, the daughter of Tarzan creator, author Edgar Rice Burroughs.

Gerard Montgomery "Monte" Blue, who played in more than 250 movies, many before talkies were introduced, was born in Indianapolis, but spent his years from eight to nearly sixteen in Knightstown at the Indiana Soldiers' and Sailors' Children's Home. His destitute mother took Blue and his brother there when their father, a Civil War veteran, died. Blue played in films with such notables as Clara Bow and Gloria Swanson. Making the switch from silent films, he appeared as a character actor in many movies and television shows and played the sheriff in the Humphrey Bogart classic *Key Largo*.

The courthouse at Covington is the only courthouse in the nation whose walls around the rotunda are covered with murals done right after the building was finished in 1937. The courthouse and the paintings, done by a crew of Fountain County artists, were a Works Progress Administration project. The murals, completed in 1940 under the direction of artist Eugene Francis Savage, cover more than 2,500 square feet. The art was restored in 1982.

Elmo Lincoln of Rochester was the first movie Tarzan and in 1922 played the role of a blacksmith in the movie *Quincy Adams Sawyer*, which starred John Bowers of Rushville and Louise Fazenda of Lafayette. Fazenda was one of Mack Sennett's bathing beauties and was one of the first Hoosiers in the movies.

According to some sources, Gary Cooper was given his stage name by his agent, who came from Gary, Indiana, although her name seems lost in history. John Wayne supposedly was named by a director in reference to Mad Anthony Wayne, in whose honor Fort Wayne is named. Who knows?

George Ade, Hoosier author, humorist, and playwright, was memorialized by a soft drink, cigar, town, hospital, country club, college football stadium, highway, interstate oasis, and Liberty ship all named in his honor. The Liberty ship was christened posthumously in August 1944.

Poet James Whitcomb Riley never owned his Indianapolis residence on Lockerbie Street, but rented quarters there from Mr. and Mrs. Charles L. Holstein. Riley's birthplace in Greenfield was built in 1850 by his father, Reuben A. Riley. Reuben, an attorney, also was a skilled craftsman and built the hand-carved walnut stairway and other features of the home. The home was sold after the Civil War and in 1883 was purchased by Riley after he achieved success as a poet.

Madelyn Davis of Indianapolis was a longtime writer for *I Love Lucy*, starring Lucille Ball, and also helped write some Ball movies, such as *Yours, Mine and Ours*, starring Ball and Henry Fonda.

The score for the film *Lord of the Flies*, released in 1963, was written by Indianapolis Symphony Orchestra director Raymond Leppard. The budget for the music in the film was extremely small, and Leppard reported making very little money from it.

Frank Sinatra made his debut with the Tommy Dorsey orchestra on February 2, 1940, on the stage of the Lyric Theater in Indianapolis.

Marjorie Main, best known as Ma Kettle in the movies, was born Marybell Tomlinson in 1890 near Acton. Main also played in *Friendly Persuasion*, written for the screen by Jessamyn West, also a Hoosier, from her own novel.

Dean Jagger, a longtime movie actor most familiar for character parts, once taught school in South Whitley and worked in a biscuit factory in Fort Wayne.

Murals were painted in thirty-seven Indiana post offices during a federal art project in the 1930s; thirty-six of them survived into the 1990s.

When the Lew Wallace novel *Ben-Hur* was filmed in 1925, among the extras cheering during the famed chariot race were Clark Gable and Myrna Loy, both would-be actors at the time, and William Wyler. Wyler directed the chariot race thirty-three years later when *Ben-Hur* was filmed again with Charlton Heston as the star.

Merrill Blosser, who developed the comic strip *Freckles and His Friends*, which appeared in newspapers all over the nation for more than fifty years (starting in 1915), was expelled from high school in Nappanee for doing caricatures of teachers that depicted the principal as a devil.

George Jean Nathan, editor, author, and critic who was born at Fort Wayne, married for the first time at the age of seventy-three.

In the 1980s Sam DeVincent, retired music director of station WOWO at Fort Wayne, gave a giant music collection to the Smithsonian Institution, representing some fifty years of collecting and including 130,000 original editions of sheet music and nearly 20,000 recordings. The songs dated to the 1790s and included very rare editions.

Catherine Winters, a nine-year-old, disappeared on March 20, 1913, from the streets of New Castle, never to be seen again. Her disappearance caused two New Castle grocers, Sylvester and Z. R. Corbett to write a song, "Where Did Catherine Winters Go?" which was played and sung all over Indiana—to no avail.

Famed broadcaster Lowell Thomas, who attended school at Northern Indiana University, now Valparaiso University, earned a bachelor's degree in two years. He enrolled in both freshman and sophomore classes during his first year, and college officials didn't find it out until midway through the semester.

There was a controversy over the burial of poet James Whitcomb Riley in Crown Hill Cemetery in Indianapolis because Greenfield, where the poet was born, wanted to be his final resting place.

Lowell Thomas.

The Sunshine Boys was the first three-act play ever performed in an adult Indiana prison when Esau Randall and Chris Cotton starred in it December 17, 1985, at the Westville Correctional Center. The play was part of a program of vocational and academic instruction.

The dedication of the Connersville High School Auditorium in 1990 as the Robert E. Wise Center for the Performing Arts honored a Hollywood producer and director who actually was born in Winchester, moving to Connersville later. Wise got his first job in Hollywood as a film porter and eventually was nominated seven times for an Academy Award, winning in 1961 for *West Side Story* and in 1965 for *The Sound of Music.*

Noted composers Harry and Albert Von Tilzer (their real name was Gumbinsky) lived in the 100 block of East Washington Street in Indianapolis, where their father operated a store of hair goods, selling wigs, false bangs, and related items. Albert wrote the words to the 1878 song "Take Me Out to the Ball Game," although he never had seen a baseball game. The song's music was written by Jack Norworth.

One of Indiana's earliest actresses was Louise Marie Fazenda of Lafayette, who appeared in some of the silent comedies of famed Hollywood director Mack Sennett. She became the wife of Warner Brothers executive Hal B. Wallis in 1927.

The *Red Skelton Show* ran on CBS from 1953 to 1970 and on NBC from 1970 to 1971, a total of seventeen years and eight months, making it among the longest running television shows of all time (so far).

A touring musical company that folded in Richmond on June 7, 1883, had among actors in an Irish melodrama L. Frank Baum, his aunt, his cousin, and his uncle. The flop of *The Maid of Arran* behind him, Baum worked at many jobs until at age forty—thirteen years after the ill-fated breakup in Richmond—he began writing children's books. His books eventually numbered seventy-nine and included *The Wizard of Oz.*

Elmer Davis of Aurora went from $10 a week on the staff of *Adventure Magazine* in 1913 to $1,000 a week in 1939 as a radio news commentator to $100 a week as the first director of the Office of War Information in 1942. He was a four-time winner of the Peabody Award, given for outstanding broadcasting. He also wrote humorous novels in the 1920s and 1930s.

In murals in the University of Notre Dame administration building, Father Thomas Walsh, president of the university from 1881 to 1893, served as the model for Columbus in one mural, and Father Edward F. Sorin, founder of the university, served as the Columbus model in another mural. The artist was Luigi Gregori, a Vatican painter who visited Notre Dame from 1874 to 1891.

George W. Whistler, father of painter James Abbott Whistler, who painted the work commonly called *Whistler's Mother*, was a Hoosier, born in Fort Wayne.

In life off the screen, Bill Crawford, longtime weatherman on early Indianapolis television, was a dentist.

The musical *Annie* was based on the comic strip *Little Orphan Annie*, which was drawn by Harold Gray, an artist who moved from Illinois to Lafayette as a child. Gray drew cartoons to finance his studies at Purdue University. When Gray died in 1986 he still was drawing the comic strip, as he had for forty-four years.

The 1949 movie *Johnny Holiday*, starring William Bendix, was filmed at the Indiana Boys School.

Hoagy Carmichael wrote a song that has a longer title than any other Hoosier-written song and may be a record for any song: "I'm a Cranky Old Yank in a Clanky Old Tank on the Streets of Yokohama with My Honolulu Mama Doin' Those Beat-o, Beat-o, Flat on My Seat-o Hirohito Blues." In addition to composing, Carmichael did an oil painting of the Corydon Constitution Elm that was hung in the Indiana Memorial Union on the Bloomington campus of Indiana University.

The Indiana song recorded the most—and one of the most recorded, period—is "Stardust," which was written by Hoagy Carmichael in Bloomington, but polished after Carmichael moved to Indianapolis. The words were written by Mitchell Parish.

Lida Carmichael, the mother of Hoagy Carmichael, played piano at sorority and fraternity dances at Indiana University in 1903–4, years before her son became a musician and songwriter in Bloomington.

Irving Berlin, one of the many celebrities to visit the French Lick hotel, composed his song "Alone" while residing there.

Robert Indiana, the artist who changed his name to honor his home state, was the star of a two-hour Andy Warhol film featuring a plate of mushrooms and titled *Eat.*

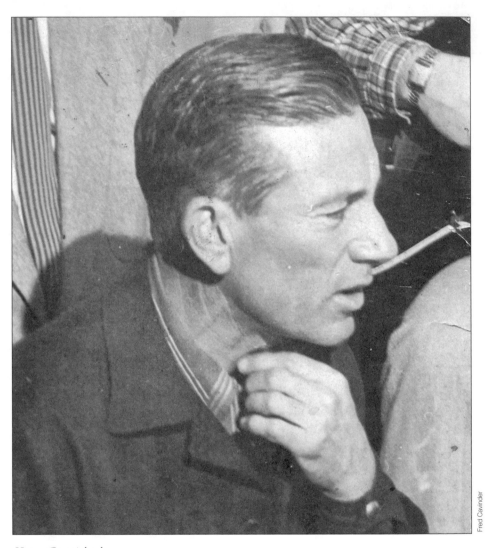

Hoagy Carmichael.

Legendary cowboy movie star Tom Mix, who joined the Sells-Floto Circus in 1929, had a suite for his horse, Tony, at the circus's Peru, Indiana, winter quarters.

Kevin Heggi, Ron Svetic, and John Swanson, all Lake County volunteer firemen, were extras who appeared in the film about firemen, *Backdraft*.

In 1925 George D. Hay, born in Attica in 1895, founded the *Grand Ole Opry*, which evolved out of a Saturday Night Jamboree in Nashville, Tennessee. The year before that Hay originated the WLS *Barn Dance*, broadcast out of Chicago. He had been a reporter in Memphis and worked at WSM Radio in Nashville.

Muncie, Indiana, was the town portrayed in the movie *Close Encounters of the Third Kind*, but the director, Steven Spielberg, never visited there.

Amalia Küssner of Terre Haute went to New York in 1892 and became a renowned painter of miniature portraits, painting the wealthiest men and women of New York and Chicago as well as such royalty as the Prince of Wales and Tsar Nicholas II of Russia. She got as much as $4,000 for a single portrait.

Before Carole Lombard (Jane Alice Peters of Fort Wayne in her Indiana days) became a noted actress and the wife of matinee idol Clark Gable, she played in thirteen Mack Sennett comedies, often taking a custard pie in the face. She appeared in her first "real" film at the age of twelve in 1921 with leading man Monte Blue, a native of Indianapolis.

Wilbur George Kurtz, who grew up in Greencastle, became a technical adviser with Selznick International Pictures and gauged the historical authenticity of vintage objects used in movies, including two million items used in *Gone with the Wind*.

When Will Hays of Sullivan and Crawfordsville became the first president of the Motion Picture Producers and Distributors of America and launched a drive to "clean up" the film industry, one result was the founding of Beverly Hills as a quiet suburb away from the glitz of Hollywood. Hays quit his post as postmaster general in the Harding administration to accept the job as "tsar" of the motion picture industry in 1922.

The first time copyright was applied to the movies was in 1901 when the Lew Wallace family took action to stop a one-reel film of *Ben-Hur*. The family won a judgment of $25,000, and movies then came under copyright protection.

When the 1959 version of the movie *Ben-Hur* was shown on television in 1971, it attracted 8.5 million viewers. Although *Ben-Hur* was surpassed in 1976 by *Gone with the Wind* when it appeared on television, the Lew Wallace story is still tops among Hoosier-related works on the tube.

Dale Harpham, who grew up in Steuben County, joined the U.S. Marine Band in 1935 and served as its director for two years before he retired in 1974. In retirement he moved to Martinsville.

Mr. Ed, the talking horse on the television show of the same name during the 1962–65 seasons, got his voice via Allan "Rocky" Lane, who was born in Mishawaka.

The exact originator of the seal of Indiana is unknown. By the time the Indiana General Assembly adopted the present seal as official in 1963, at least two hundred variations had been made.

When the Indianapolis Soldiers and Sailors Monument was dedicated in 1902, music was written for the occasion by famed bandsman John Philip Sousa to words written by noted Indiana poet James Whitcomb Riley. It was called "Messiah of the Nations."

The first female collaborators to have a show reach Broadway in New York were songwriter Nancy Ford and lyricist Gretchen Cryer, Hoosiers who wrote *Shelter* in 1973.

Paul Dresser birthplace.

Paul Dresser of Terre Haute was said to have read the words he had composed for "On the Banks of the Wabash, Far Away" at a dinner in 1897 at Mudlavia, a spa in Warren County; it was the first public introduction of the song.

Songwriter Paul Dresser, who wrote "On the Banks of the Wabash, Far Away" and "My Gal Sal," studied for the priesthood. It is said that "My Gal Sal" referred to Sallie Walker, who ran a brothel Dresser frequented during the time he lived in Evansville in the 1880s.

When it came time to paint the official portrait of Indiana governor Evan Bayh, a practice begun in 1869 by Governor Conrad Baker, forty artists applied for the commission. The job went to Michael Chelich of Munster.

Two of the most active composers of ragtime music in Indianapolis were women—Julia Lee Niebergall and May Frances Aufderheide.

Clifton Webb, the Indianapolis native known for his roles in the films *Laura, Mr. Belvedere,* and many others, was a professional dancer at age nineteen, performing with partner Bonnie Glass. He abandoned that career to appear in silent films in the 1920s.

Carter's Tavern in Indianapolis gave the state's first theatrical performance, a presentation of "solemn" music played by an orchestra of one violin.

In the 1980s and 1990s the Convent of the Immaculate Conception in Ferdinand made religious habits to rent to high schools and theaters that were presenting plays and musicals involving nuns, such as *The Sound of Music.* The costumes were made in the convent's clothing shop and rented all over Indiana and to theater groups in other states.

Irene Dunne, who grew up in Madison, was nominated for an Academy Award for best actress five times, but never won. She also was the first woman named to the board of directors of Technicolor Inc. and was an alternate delegate to the United Nations.

The Butler University's collection of material on composer Jean Sibelius is the largest outside his native Finland and was donated to the Indianapolis school by a collector.

James Whitcomb Riley died before Indianapolis artist Myra Richards completed sculpting a statue of Riley for the Greenfield Courthouse lawn. Consequently, actor John Drew posed for the completion of Riley's body from the waist down on the statue, dedicated in 1918.

The publication of "You've Been a Good Old Wagon but You Done Broke Down" by Bruner Greenup at Evansville in 1895 may have been the nation's first printing of a song in the syncopated rhythm of ragtime.

The Circle Theater Company in Indianapolis founded First National Studios in Hollywood in the early days of the movies; the studio later became Warner Brothers.

In 1950 the U.S. State Department *Voice of America* broadcast chose Delphi as a typical midwestern city; what this did for Delphi seems unrecorded.

Probably the most famous item in the Goodwin Museum, a private exhibit at the Goodwin Funeral Home in Frankfort, was the old Maxwell automobile that belonged to radio and television star Jack Benny. But it was rivaled by one of the cars driven in the film *The Great Race*.

The real first name of Phil Harris, who was born in Linton, was Wonga. It was the name of an Indian chief Phil's father had known in a circus.

William J. Haney, who operated a movie theater and restaurant in Milan for twenty-five years, is said to have invented metal taps and mats used in tap dancing. He was in vaudeville more than twenty years.

Gordon Gordon, a native of Anderson, and his wife Mildred wrote a book called *Mystery Cat* that Disney made into a movie in 1963 called *That Darned Cat*.

Dale Messick, creator of the long-running comic strip *Brenda Starr*, was born Dalia Messick in 1906 in South Bend, but changed her name to Dale because she felt editors were prejudiced against female cartoonists.

Not only was Charles Francis Jenkins, resident of Wayne County from 1870 to 1886, a pioneer in motion pictures, he also invented the conical paper cup and pioneered in television by transmitting weather maps to ships at sea in the 1920s.

The Damm family, which operated a bakery and the Damm Theater in Osgood, charged a nickel or twenty wrappers from Damm Bread as admission to the theater after it opened in 1914.

Fred Shaffer, a native of Clinton County, played trumpet in such noted bands as those of Fred Waring and Paul Whiteman until returning to Clinton County to teach

Damm Theater.

music in the schools. In 1938 he organized an all-girl band that played at dances and on tours, including two years on USO tours, beginning in 1943 as the Victory Sweethearts, to entertain servicemen. Shaffer discontinued the band in 1953.

Ralph Boice made movie history during the Great Depression when he decided newsreels were too expensive to rent and show in his Strand Theater in Warsaw. He began filming his own newsreels of events in the area and showed them on the Strand screen. The films increased attendance among local moviegoers eager to see themselves in the news.

Sculptor John Angus Chamberlain, descendant of the founder of Rochester, Indiana, created art by tying foam rubber around various shapes. When his artwork was shipped to Pittsburgh for an exhibit, museum personnel cut the strings holding the foam rubber to seek the artwork they thought the foam rubber was protecting.

The Notre Dame victory march was created in 1908 by Michael Shea, a music instructor at the university, and his brother, John, a graduate student. Michael later became a priest, and John worked in government in Massachusetts.

Russell P. Harker, Indiana University student and director of the IU band, wrote the IU fight song, "Indiana, Our Indiana," and published it in 1913. He became an attorney in Frankfort, served in the Indiana General Assembly, and received the IU Distinguished Alumni Award in 1966.

Edward J. Wotawa already had graduated from Purdue University in 1914 when he wrote the music for "Hail, Hail to Old Purdue" to words written by James Morrison. Wotawa became a teacher and ran the music department at the University of Louisville. Morrison became a journalist working for the *New York Herald* and United Press.

Carl Hofer wrote the Ball State University fight song in 1930 on a dare by his younger sister to prove he was a musician. He won a twenty-five dollar prize for the best pep song for the school.

The role of Baby Patsy May was played by Doris May Dittemore of Gosport in the 1930s in the Our Gang comedies with Spanky McFarland, Buckwheat, and others.

Walter O. Miles, who grew up in Union City, got into the movies after he was sixty years old. He began by appearing in radio dramas and then was in numerous television roles. He was chief radar dispatcher in the movie *Close Encounters of the Third Kind* and played General Kenney in *MacArthur*. Before deciding to try acting, Miles was in the printing business in California.

A theater in Earl Park defied the Indiana blue law prohibiting the showing of movies on Sundays. In a historic court case in 1922 the theater won its case, claiming the blue law was improper, but the victory, which permitted larger towns to show movies on the Sabbath, caused the Earl Park theater to close because of lack of customers.

J. P. McEvoy and John H. Striebel met at the University of Notre Dame as students and years later, in 1931, created *Dixie Dugan*, the first continuity comic strip in the United States. Striebel was the son of a South Bend grocer; McEvoy was a New Yorker.

The decorative painting of the Federal Building in Indianapolis, considered a mural, is the largest in Indiana and among the largest in the world. The blended tones of shocking pastels were created by New York designer Milton Glaser in 1974. Hoosiers who were not enthralled with the mural blamed local architect Evans Woollen, who had nothing to do with it.

The Maennerchor, a singing group in Indianapolis founded in 1854, is the oldest continuously performing male chorus in the United States.

In 1985 Dan Britton of Bloomfield became documented as the lowest singer in the world, at least as long as his voice held out. Britton was singing bass with the Britton Brothers country band. He was shown to sing four Es below middle C. At the time the world's lowest was only three Cs below middle C, six notes higher than Britton.

The concert of Hoosier John Cougar Mellencamp at Market Square Arena in Indianapolis for December 15 and 16, 1985, sold out the first show, 17,626 seats, in fifty-five minutes.

Will Geer, born in New Hope and raised at Frankfort and noted as a movie actor and as the grandfather on the television series *The Waltons*, had a master's degree in botany from Columbia University.

Automotive

Mary E. Landon is believed to be the first woman to drive a car, in 1899 at Kokomo. She was the cousin of Elmer Apperson, founder of the Haynes-Apperson Wagon Company. She was also an employee of the firm and gave up driving quickly because she said the roads were too crowded.

When Tarlton Kenworthy, twenty-eight years old, died instantly in a crash on the morning of April 28, 1907, while racing with a second car en route to see a train wreck at Winchester, it was thought to be the first traffic fatality in the United States. Kenworthy struck a dog in the road and veered into a tree, dying of a broken neck. Ironically, Kenworthy operated a garage and sold Reos, one of the newfangled automobiles. No one was hurt in the train wreck the two cars were racing to see. Four men riding with Kenworthy were hurt: E. R. Hiatt, who later was killed in an auto crash in Florida; J. A. Edwards; W. P. Marlott; and J. W. Ruby.

Although Auburn is widely known today as a producer of early cars in Indiana, Connersville is little remembered for actually making seven early autos, including some associated with Auburn—Lexington, Empire, Howard, Van Auken, Ansted, Cord, and Auburn.

Autos have been manufactured in more than fifty cities in Indiana. More than two hundred makes of cars have been built in Indiana. When trucks, motorcycles, and cyclecars are added to the list, the cities and towns making them number eighty-eight with more than five hundred varieties of vehicles involved.

Only Indianapolis was the manufacturing site of more automobile makes than Elkhart, where twenty-seven makes were produced.

Earl "Lucky" Teeter, a daredevil from Noblesville, planned to join the army in 1942, but agreed to do one more thrill show at the Indiana State Fairgrounds. He crashed and was killed in the show July 5.

Two Indiana motoring pioneers were A. T. Mosher and Harry Harter, both of Anderson, who drove six thousand miles in 1908–9 from Anderson through Kentucky, Tennessee, and Georgia into Florida, then to New Orleans and Mississippi and through

Illinois back to Indiana. Their goal over rudimentary roads was to demonstrate the efficiency of the new Remy automobile magneto, developed at Anderson.

The first privately purchased car in Indianapolis is believed to have been one bought by Carl Fisher, who, in 1904, circled a two-mile dirt track in a record two minutes.

The Maxwell motor car, which was immortalized as the car driven by radio comedian Jack Benny, was built at the Maxwell-Briscoe plant in New Castle beginning in 1907.

A compact economy car, belt driven and built in 1914 at the Auburn plant of the McIntyre Company, sold for $375 and was called the Imp.

Indiana was the first state to enact a drunk-driving law, based on chemical tests using devices developed by Doctor Rolla Harger, inventor of the Drunkometer.

A major work that brought the automobile to the forefront in America was *A Hoosier Holiday*, written in 1916 by Theodore Dreiser, who recorded a car trip from New York City to his hometown of Terre Haute. The five-hundred-page work was called a "high tide in Dreiser's writing."

A miniature auto developed by Powell Crosley Jr. and made in Indiana had its debut June 19, 1939, in the basement of Macy's department store in New York City. Crosley was a wealthy landowner whose extensive holdings on the Muscatatuck River became part of the Crosley State Fish and Wildlife Area. He had developed small cars earlier, but the ventures failed. His 1939 two-cylinder model and others developed after World War II clashed with America's love for big cars, and the Marion plant ceased automobile production in 1952.

Fred Newlin Jr. of Crawfordsville was struck and injured by his own car while standing near an intersection in Lafayette. The auto had been stolen a short time earlier and swerved out of control as the thief fled. The car was found abandoned about half a block from where Newlin was struck.

In September 1948 a group of Tucker automobiles drove around the Indianapolis Motor Speedway track for ten days to two weeks to test the suspension, oil consumption, handling, and economy. Preston T. Tucker, builder of the ill-fated Tucker, was a sponsor of Indianapolis race cars and a friend of then Speedway president Wilbur Shaw. No record was kept of the testing. Tucker lost his car plant in Chicago, and the Tucker car ended in 1950.

When Elwood Haynes tried out his horseless carriage outside Kokomo it was towed to the test site by horses.

Aviation

Orville and Wilbur Wright, aviation pioneers, did not finish school.

Before they developed an airplane, the Wright brothers made the world's first wind tunnel, where they compiled figures usable in designing a plane that could fly.

The glider that the Wright brothers built for experimental flight at Kitty Hawk in 1900 contained material costing about fifteen dollars, according to one biographer. While experimenting at Kitty Hawk, Orville did the cooking, and Wilbur washed the dishes.

When Wilbur Wright arrived in Elizabeth City, North Carolina, in September 1900, and sought a way to get to Kitty Hawk, the first person he asked had never heard of the place. When he hired a boat to take him there from the mainland for glider experiments, it took two days to sail the forty miles, partly because of headwinds. The trip would take minutes by air today.

The first airplane flight of the Wright brothers in 1903 received very little publicity. It was not until May 1908 that newspaper reporters came to realize the significance of the Wrights' flight.

In a poll taken by the Associated Press, the Wright brothers and the growth of aviation were named among the twenty most important events in U.S. history.

Katherine Wright, sister of Orville and Wilbur, lived with Orville in Dayton, Ohio, after Wilbur died of typhoid in 1912. She married *Kansas City Star* editor Henry Haskell when she was fifty-two and died three years later. Planes from

Wright Patterson Field dropped flowers when she was buried beside Wilbur in Woodlawn Cemetery in Dayton.

George W. Steele Jr. of Marion crossed the Atlantic Ocean in a dirigible four years before Charles Lindbergh did it in an airplane and became an international celebrity at the time.

Arthur Smith, nineteen years old, and Aimee Cour left Fort Wayne on October 12, 1912, and flew seventy-five miles to Hillsdale College in Michigan. They became the first couple to elope by airplane. They flew in a biplane and stopped once for gas.

Lawrence D. Bell, an aviation pioneer, who served early as a mechanic for his brother Grover Bell, an exhibition flier who died in a crash, hated and feared to fly. He was born in 1894 at Mentone, where a museum details his contributions to aviation. Bell designed the first jet-propelled plane in 1944 at a plant in Buffalo, New York, which employed numerous workers from Kosciusko County. Bell also designed planes that set speed and altitude records, and his Bell Aircobra was a highly rated fighter plane in World War II.

An airfield, Schoen Field, once occupied the site where the Army Finance Center at Fort Benjamin Harrison in Indianapolis was later located.

Roderick Wright of Washington, Indiana, a barnstormer and later a test pilot, served as a pallbearer at the funeral in 1948 of aviation pioneer Orville Wright. They were unrelated, but Orville had taught Roderick to fly.

Hickam Air Force Base in Hawaii was named in honor of Colonel Horace D. Hickam, an aviator from Spencer who lost his life in a Texas aircraft crash in 1934.

The Purdue University collection of material on Amelia Earhart, who once was a part-time career counselor at the West Lafayette campus, is surpassed only by one other collection on the ill-fated aviatrix—that of Radcliffe College.

Some wanted the airplane of Amelia Earhart, which had been purchased by the Purdue Research Foundation with the help of private funds, to be trimmed in

Lawrence D. Bell.

black and gold, the Purdue University colors. However, orange was settled on for its greater visibility. Earhart, who had been a counselor at Purdue from 1935 to 1937, left in July 1937 for a trip around the world to gather data on what was called the Purdue Flying Laboratory. She vanished in the Pacific Ocean.

An army flying facility with hangars and a landing strip was established during World War I inside the Indianapolis Motor Speedway, and a camp was built along

THE INDIANA BOOK OF TRIVIA

the railroad off Main Street in the town of Speedway for 650 soldiers who rebuilt and tested planes.

When Arthur Roy Smith of Fort Wayne, an aviation pioneer, needed an engine for his first plane in 1910, his parents mortgaged their home to get the $350 purchase price. Smith starred as a daredevil and skywriter and later flew the mail.

The Indianapolis heliport, opened in May 1985, was the nation's first full-service downtown facility and served as a model for some other heliports. It cost $2.3 million and could handle twenty-five helicopters at once.

When an air show was held in 1910 at the Indianapolis Motor Speedway (before the 500-mile race was born), three airplanes nearly were lost—because they were shipped by rail. The planes came from the training grounds of the Wright brothers at Montgomery, Alabama. The planes finally were found aboard freight cars in the Indianapolis railroad yards in time for the show. The air show, in which airplanes competed for such things as altitude records, was the first licensed air show in America.

The first airplane altitude record was set in a June 1910 air show at the Indianapolis Motor Speedway when Walter S. Brookins, using a Wright airplane, rose to 4,384½ feet. The next day he reached 4,938 feet.

Art Smith, an Adams County pioneer flier, was the first in the nation to fly at night, do skywriting, and set off fireworks from a plane; in 1916 he was dubbed the most daring aviator in America. He lost his life in 1926 while carrying the mail.

The first air-mail deliveries in Indiana were conducted by flights hopping between Connersville, Rushville, Evansville, and Rockport.

The first death of a pilot delivering the mail happened in Indiana on March 10, 1920, when Clayton Stoner's aircraft burned near New Paris on the Chicago-Cleveland air route. It was believed that Stoner became lost in the fog and sought the Wabash Railroad to guide him. The plane hit trees in the woods, and the gas tank exploded.

The last surviving letter from a Jupiter balloon flight from Lafayette to Crawfordsville, the first attempt to deliver letters by air, was purchased at auction by the Smithsonian Institution for $6,500 in 1920. Mailed to Mary A. Wells, it was one of 146 pieces of mail carried by John Wise in the balloon ascension on August 17, 1859. The letter had been in the collection of Thomas A. Matthews of Ohio. Wise had planned to reach New York, but winds took him to Crawfordsville instead. The mail completed the journey by rail.

John Anthony, a Martin County farmer, made Indiana aviation history in 1875 by building wings that attached to his arms and flapping them while jumping off a barn. He crashed. Later he built a more conventional and more successful glider.

Ellen Church, one of seven nurses hired by United Airlines as the world's first stewardesses, was turned down in her request in 1930 to become a pilot for Boeing Air Transport Command. She later was an administrator at Union Hospital in Terre Haute.

Purdue University's airport, opened in 1932, was the first university airport in the nation.

In June 1935, when the Farmland Airport was opened, pilot Clyde Shockley went aloft to set off celebratory fireworks from an airplane, but bailed out when the fireworks caught fire in the cockpit.

When the dirigible LZ-3, built by the German government and turned over to the United States as part of World War I reparations, was flown from Germany to New Jersey, two observers on board were Hoosiers—Lieutenant Commander Sydney M. Kraus of Peru and Captain George W. Steele Jr., whose father was a congressman from the old Indiana Eleventh District.

Albert Rupel of Jay County built a successful glider-plane in 1904, but his life as a potential Indiana aviation pioneer ended when he stepped on a nail a year later, developed tetanus, and died.

Captain G. L. Bumbaugh's The Indianapolis Star was at one time the largest dirigible built in the United States. It carried a Stoddard-Dayton automobile over Indianapolis as a promotion.

Octave Chanute, who was a consultant to the Wright brothers of aviation fame, performed numerous glider tests at sand dunes where the city of Gary now stands.

One of Indiana's earliest students of aeronautical science was Albert Zahm, a student at Notre Dame, who built several craft designed to fly. Zahm became chief of the aeronautical division of the Library of Congress and was considered Indiana's first well-trained aeronautical engineer.

Octave Chanute.

Helen Montgomery of the Fort Wayne area set records for women in glider endurance, altitude, and distance.

Hoosier pilots Jack Schweibold, R. Frederick "Fritz" Harvey, and Harry B. Sutton set fifteen records for commercial helicopters in a seven-thousand-mile, two-day flight over the United States and Canada in April 1985. They flew a Sikorsky S-76 Mark II, a thirty-five-foot craft with an Allison engine. Records included coast-to-coast (New York to Los Angeles with three fuel stops), nonstop, altitude, and speed.

In 1940 a site for training airplane mechanics for national defense was set up at the Indiana State Fairgrounds in Indianapolis; up to a thousand mechanics were trained every month.

In 1892 the Brightwood Aerial Navigation Company was formed in Indianapolis, but the members met in secret because at that time believers in flying machines were considered "a little cracked." W. A. Mercer, who was the group's airship designer, created a craft that flew, but he went crazy—crashed the ship and burned the plans.

When Mitch Hudson, fourteen years and two months old, took his glider up at Terry Field near Zionsville on August 15, 1991, he became the youngest person ever to solo in a glider.

Bridges

The only surviving two-lane covered bridge in Indiana is that at the entrance to Brown County State Park. It was built in 1838 by Henry Wolfe, moved to the park from Putnam County in 1932, and restored in 1969.

Indiana's first covered bridge was a span across Symons Creek where it crossed the National Road west of Dublin in Henry County. It was erected in 1834 and demolished in 1921.

The last covered bridge to span the Wabash River, the Ceylon Covered Bridge near Berne, no longer stands on the river channel. Closed to traffic in 1948, it is part of the Limberlost Park.

A portion of the huge Ferris wheel that was erected at the World's Columbian Exhibition in Chicago in 1893 and used at the Saint Louis World's Fair in 1904 became a bridge over the Kankakee River at Tefft in Jasper County. The bridge was sold for scrap after the world's fair, and a section was bought by Isaac Dunn, a farmer from the Tefft area. The bridge was closed to traffic by the late 1970s.

The small image of a bridge printed on Hoosier vehicle titles is a span in Crawford County honored because in 1938, the year of its completion, it was the first bridge in Indiana that not only curved, but also sloped. It spans a rail line near the village of Milltown.

The covered bridge south of Williams in Lawrence County is the longest still in use in Indiana, a span of 402 feet.

Sometimes the Huffman Mill Covered Bridge near Saint Meinrad was half painted and half unpainted because the span is half owned by Spencer County and half owned by Perry County.

The shortest public covered bridge in Indiana is the forty-three-foot Phillips Covered Bridge in Parke County. It was built by J. A. Britton in 1909.

Dunn's Bridge, Kankakee River.

Crime and Criminals

Sam Bass, born near Buddha, Lawrence County, to Daniel and Elizabeth Bass, was a deputy working for the sheriff in Denton, Texas, in the 1870s before he was lured into banditry by easy money, beginning with a scam involving a racehorse of which he was co-owner. He was killed in 1878 at the age of twenty-seven after five years as a noted western badman. His grave in Round Rock, Texas, has as the tombstone inscription: "A brave man reposes in death here. Why was he not true?" The log cabin of Bass's grandfather is part of the Spring Mill State Park Pioneer Village, used as the weaver's home.

The first Indianapolis policeman killed in the line of duty, Charles Ware, was shot while involved in a battle with a miscreant at New Jersey and Georgia streets on April 28, 1897. Ware arrived at the scene of the dispute on a bicycle.

The section of the jail adjacent to the Jefferson County Courthouse is the oldest intact jail in Indiana, dating back to the creation of the courthouse in 1848.

Richard Dillinger, half brother of bank robber John Dillinger, worked as a mechanic for the Indiana State Police. Richard's sister Ethel also worked for the state police as a secretary.

Legend is that John Dillinger buried $200,000 in the woods near Little Bohemia roadhouse in Wisconsin in late April 1934 while escaping a shoot-out, but the money never has been found.

John Dillinger and his gang never robbed a bank at Marion because, a gang member said, the streets are too narrow and the blocks too long for a good getaway.

It was said that John Dillinger used the Baron Lamm method in robbing banks. The term came from Herman K. "Baron" Lamm, a Prussian-born former army officer. Lamm employed the meticulous precision of a military campaign in planning his robberies.

In 1924 bank robber John Dillinger played shortstop on the baseball team at the Indiana State Prison. Earlier that year he had played on a team from Martinsville, Indiana.

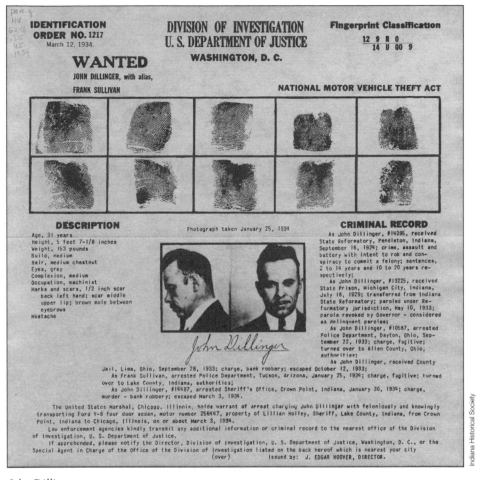

John Dillinger.

Among reasons some contended that John Dillinger was not really killed outside the Biograph Theater in Chicago is that the corpse allegedly had brown eyes and Dillinger's eyes were gray. It was claimed by some that the body of a hoodlum named James Lawrence was passed off as that of Dillinger.

Bank robber John Dillinger was buried in Crown Hill Cemetery in Indianapolis in 1934 over the protests of many who owned plots in the cemetery.

George W. Barrett was hanged in the Marion County jail on March 24, 1936, for murdering federal agent Nelson Bernard Klein in College Corner. Barrett was the first man hanged under a 1934 law making killing a federal officer a capital offense.

Robert T. Humes of Indianapolis was named July 15, 1921, to head the new Motor Vehicle Police Department, which later developed into the Indiana State Police. The vehicle police, consisting of sixteen men, had the sole responsibility of apprehending car thieves.

Bert Scott was the first president of the first Jaycee chapter organized in a federal prison, the Wabash Valley Jaycee chapter in the federal penitentiary at Terre Haute, established March 10, 1967.

In Gary, after the sprawling city was founded in 1906, with its lonely woods, sand hills, and sloughs, police handcuffed drunks, somewhat plentiful in a booming but isolated town, to available trees or saplings. They were collected from time to time with the city's rented gray mare and buckboard for transfer to the two-cell jail.

Lewis Weichman, a student in Maryland who became a friend of John Suratt, was the main witness against members of the Suratt family accused of conspiring in the assassination of President Abraham Lincoln. Fearing retaliation for his testimony, Weichman moved to Anderson, founded Anderson Business College, and never overcame his fears until he died June 5, 1902, in Anderson.

On May 22, 1868, a year and a half after its first train robbery, the Reno gang pulled its most lucrative crime, taking $96,000 from a train at Marshfield Station south of Austin.

In one of the most famous lynchings in Indiana history, residents of Seymour forced their way into the New Albany jail in 1868, seized four members of the Reno gang, and hanged them. The Renos had committed the nation's first robbery of a moving train in 1866 near Seymour. Those hanged were Frank, William, and Simeon Reno and Charlie Anderson.

Abe Smith and Tom Shipp were the two black teenagers lynched on August 7, 1930, at Marion in one of Indiana's greatest twentieth-century criminal tragedies.

Jimmy Hoffa, born in Brazil, disappeared July 30, 1975, outside a Michigan restaurant with foul play suspected and is known as Missing Person 75-3425.

Ernest Tait is one of the few criminals to make the FBI ten most wanted list twice. In 1951 he made it the first time for burglarizing the New Castle Elks Lodge with another burglar. Arrested in twenty-four hours, he was sentenced to two to five years. In 1960, free from prison, he made the list a second time for burglary. He was captured again.

Sile Doty, a native of Vermont, moved west to continue his lifelong activities of stealing horses and anything else he could, often giving his ill-gotten gains to those who needed them and sometimes stealing "on order." He stole lumber and nails for the first Baptist Church at Clear Lake in Steuben County.

Women felons were forced to bathe weekly in an open-air reservoir at the Indiana State Reformatory, then at Jeffersonville, until an 1868 report to the governor by a group of Quaker women led to a separate prison for women. It opened in Indianapolis late in 1873.

James Jenkins, a member of the John Dillinger gang, was shot to death outside McDonald's Grocery in Bean Blossom in 1933 after he hitchhiked to Brown County from the prison at Michigan City. Jenkins shot the Bean Blossom grocer in the shoulder and got a fatal shot in return from one of the grocer's neighbors.

Belle Brynhilde Gunness, notorious for marrying and killing suitors at her farm near La Porte, was married to Mads Sorenson before she became Belle Gunness by marrying Peter Gunness, a fellow Norwegian. Sorenson died suspiciously of an "enlarged heart," and Belle collected $8,500 on his insurance. Later, Peter Gunness also died when a heavy sausage grinder fell on his head. His death brought Belle $4,000 in insurance.

The son of Belle and Peter Gunness was born after Peter died. At that time Belle also had three adopted children, Jenny, Myrtle, and Lucy, acquired while she was married to Mads Sorenson in Chicago.

Belle Gunness bought her farm near La Porte with money she got from the insurance on her confectionery store in Chicago, which burned.

Although weighing some two hundred pounds, toothless, and penniless, Belle Gunness lured her victims with advertisements in matrimonial journals such as this one: "Comely widow who owns a large farm in one of the finest districts in LaPorte County, Indiana, desires to make acquaintance of gentleman equally well provided, with a view of joining fortunes. No replies by letter considered unless sender is willing to follow answer with a personal visit."

The first conviction in Indiana and possibly in the United States of a man charged with attempting to kill by transmitting the AIDS virus to another was that of Donald J. Haines, age thirty-three, in January 1988 at Lafayette. He was found to have tried to infect a policeman and two medical technicians with AIDS by spitting, biting, and throwing his blood.

The jail in Vevay, built in 1857 and thought to be the oldest in the state, is so primitive that in the 1990s the circuit court judge would not permit prisoners to be kept there longer than three days. After three days they were moved across the Ohio River to facilities in Kentucky.

Inmates of the Indiana State Prison began making state license plates in 1930, a job they continued for more than fifty years.

Souvenir hunters seeking mementos of a hanging at Versailles in 1897 were so avid that one dug a bullet from the body of Lyle Levi, one of the victims, who was shot before being hanged.

At Chesterton in the 1920s and 1930s the town marshal patrolled on foot. To call police, citizens called the telephone operator. She turned on a flashing red light that was over a room she occupied and was atop the M. Smith and Son store. The light alerted the town marshal that he was wanted on the phone.

Maybe crime does pay, for some. An impressive two-story house at 503 West Sixth Street in Seymour was built in 1875 by William T. Branaman, who was an attorney for the Reno family, some of whose members committed the first robbery of a moving train.

Lucile Myers was the first Hoosier female police officer killed in the line of duty when, in 1926, as a Lake County juvenile court patrol officer, she went to a home to check on nine children living in "deplorable conditions." She was shot in the head by the enraged father of the children.

William Dudley Pelley was found guilty August 6, 1942, in Indianapolis on eleven counts of sedition for aiding the Nazi Party through articles in the magazine *Gililean*, which he published. It was the first major sedition conviction of World War II. Pelley got fifteen years in the federal penitentiary at Terre Haute, was paroled in 1950, and lived in retirement in Noblesville until his death in 1965 at the age of seventy-five.

Famed lawyer Clarence Darrow of Chicago defended four men in the Kosciusko County Courthouse at Warsaw who were charged with robbing the bank at Culver and killing a policeman. All four were convicted in the 1921 trial and were sentenced to life.

An all-female jury, the first in Indiana, decided a case at Vernon on June 6, 1921, and found B. B. Cox innocent of threatening George Russell. Members were Mrs. M. J. Benson, Maggie Abbott, Mrs. E. P. Trapp, Mrs. Jessie Richardson, Mrs. Kate Wenzel, Mrs. Anna Hengstler, Mrs. Zelpha Webber, Mrs. Nellie Long, Mrs. Isabelle Waltermire, Mrs. Myra Culp, Mrs. Louise W. Barth, and Mrs. Mary Stemm.

D. C. Stephenson, convicted of second degree murder in the death of Madge Oberholtzer and sentenced to life imprisonment, was paroled twice. Governor Henry F. Schricker granted him a parole in 1950 with the provision that he take a job in Carbondale, Illinois, and remain there. When Stephenson showed up in Minneapolis, the parole was revoked. Governor George N. Craig granted Stephenson a parole and discharge from prison in 1956. Stephenson moved to Seymour, Indiana.

Glendon R. Wininger of Bloomington was sentenced to eight years in prison for killing her boyfriend, Steven M. Detmer, on January 4, 1985, by dropping a fourteen-pound bowling ball repeatedly on his head after what she said was a series of beatings by Detmer.

A car show at the federal penitentiary at Terre Haute in September 1992 to raise money for needy families was the first in a federal prison in Indiana and only the second in the nation. The first had been held at Lewisburg Penitentiary and was the idea of Warden Patrick W. Keohane, who had moved from Lewisburg to Terre Haute.

The first judge in Indiana convicted and sentenced for a federal offense was Orval W. Anderson, sixty years old, given three years for perjury on August 2, 1985, after being found guilty as a jurist in Lake County of lying in the trial of a bailiff and another man in a case of payoffs in drunk-driving cases. He had resigned after his conviction at Lafayette.

Virginia Caming of Fort Wayne was a court reporter at the Nuremberg trials in which Nazis were tried for crimes committed during World War II. Caming, who graduated from Fort Wayne North Side High School, became a stenographer and worked for Judge Edward Meyers of Allen County. She got the job at Nuremberg after seeing an advertisement in a newspaper at Cincinnati for court reporters for the war trials.

A computer designed to test for the use of alcohol, marijuana, and cocaine was first tried in Indiana by the Bartholomew County Sheriff's office. Called Veritas, the equipment used electrodes to the temple to examine brain waves. If such screening showed use of those substances it was followed up by laboratory tests.

Bettie L. Higgins Shaffer, who owned Aid Detective Agency in Indianapolis for twenty-two years, was the first registered and bonded private detective in Indiana. She also was a detective for L. Strauss and Company, an Indianapolis department store.

Culture

Independence Day activities in Indianapolis in 1900 included a head-on crash between two railroad locomotives in front of the grandstand at the Indiana State Fairgrounds. Onlookers said the engines were going about twenty-five miles an hour when they collided.

Kilsoquah, granddaughter of Little Turtle, had a home in Roanoke, Indiana, and lived among whites most of her life, but never learned English; her son, Anthony Revarre, acted as her interpreter.

Joseph Bailly, a French Canadian fur trader who settled in La Porte County in 1822, translated the New Testament into the Potawatomi language.

When Jenny Lind, the coloratura known as the Swedish Nightingale, came to Madison her concert was staged in a pork slaughterhouse.

When John T. Brush was met by delay after delay in remodeling his store building in Indianapolis, he took out newspaper ads saying "When," a reference to the date the store would be able to open. When it did, it was called the When Store.

Joaquin Miller of Liberty, who became known as a California forest preservationist and poet, said he got his poetic inspiration from whiskey. He lived in Fulton County from 1848 to 1852 before going west.

It is said that in days gone by, a house in Elkinsville in the Hoosier National Forest in Brown County had a sign in front, possibly aimed at tourists, which read: "No telephone, water, information, towing, hunting, hiking, fishing, trespassing, etc. Keep Out."

During Prohibition, a temperance advocate named Mrs. Johnson attached a pair of oxen to pillars before a tavern at Mansfield and pulled the bar into the creek.

In Ferdinand many residents spoke German until World War II.

Sarah La Tourette, when taught by her father John to quilt at Covington, became the first known woman professional quilter in Indiana; most professional quilters were men in those early days.

Reverend Charles Leo O'Donnell, a native of Greenfield and in later years president of the University of Notre Dame, was the first president of the Catholic Poetry Society of America.

There were at least twenty-two recorded experiments with communal societies in Indiana. None of them succeeded for any length of time.

By 1900 Indiana had more Quakers than any other state, making Indiana a world center of Quakers.

Circa 1917, artist William A. Baxter of Anderson, a speed painter, did about five thousand versions of the old swimming hole at Greenfield, which had been memorialized by James Whitcomb Riley in his poem, "The Old Swimmin' Hole," written in 1882. None of the five thousand paintings was exactly alike.

In August 1954 Earl Wiley Bottomlee asked the Orange County Circuit Court to change his name to Aearlygodlet Wileyelectronspirit Leegravity. The judge said no because it "would be against public policy."

May Wright Sewall, who lived in Franklin and Indianapolis, founded or cofounded more than fifty local, national, and international organizations between the 1870s and her death in 1920 in Indianapolis. Many of the groups were involved in women's rights.

Robert Dale Owen, while he was a congressman from Indiana, introduced the bill creating the Smithsonian Institution.

For some years the variety store in Rising Sun piped music throughout the downtown business district. The custom stopped in 1990 when Les Fogel's five-and-dime store was taken over by a telemarketing firm.

Every known barn in Indiana that had a Mail Pouch tobacco sign, a total of more than 250, was photographed by bank official Thomas L. Plimpton of Indianapolis.

Will Shortz, a native of Crawfordsville, became editor of *Games* magazine in the mid-1980s, quite possibly because he held a degree in enigmatology (study of puzzles or riddles).

During the 1920s between 25 percent and 35 percent of all native Hoosier men joined the Ku Klux Klan. Many women also joined Women of the Ku Klux Klan.

William Maclure, who founded the Workingmen's Institute at New Harmony to bring useful knowledge to laborers there, left an estate when he died in 1840 that funded 144 libraries in Indiana.

Part of the land occupied by the Indianapolis Central Library (the present-day Indianapolis–Marion County Public Library) was donated by poet James Whitcomb Riley.

The first newspaper in Porter County measured a mere twelve by six inches. It was called the *Republican* and was founded by James Castle in Valparaiso.

Ray Geiger, longtime editor of *The Farmer's Almanac*, received a degree in philosophy from the University of Notre Dame.

The birthplace of John Hay, Secretary of State under presidents William McKinley and Theodore Roosevelt, was built as the Salem Grammar School. The school was operated by John Irwin Morrison, whose daughter Sarah Morrison was the first woman to enroll in and to graduate from Indiana University.

The first woman named to the Indiana Journalism Hall of Fame was Helene Foellinger, honored in 1974; the Foellinger family published the *Fort Wayne News-Sentinel* from 1920 to 1981.

One of the early newspapers in Jay County was called *Bazoo*; it started in 1886.

When campaigning against alcohol, writer Upton Sinclair listed four Hoosiers among celebrities who were heavy drinkers: author Theodore Dreiser and Socialist Party founder Eugene V. Debs, both of Terre Haute; poet of the Sierras Joaquin Miller of Liberty; and journalist-pundit Ambrose Bierce, who grew up in Warsaw.

Radio station WOZ in Richmond, operated by the Richmond newspaper of the time, the *Palladium*, was the first station in Indiana to broadcast regular farm news, beginning in 1921.

Potawatomi chief Simon Pokagon attended Notre Dame Preparatory School in South Bend at the age of fourteen and also attended Oberlin College in Ohio. He wrote and spoke on Native American subjects. His father, Leopold Pokagon, sold about one million acres, including the site of Chicago, to the government for three dollars an acre. Their memories are honored in the name of Pokagon State Park.

Eugene V. Debs.

THE INDIANA BOOK OF TRIVIA

Henry Ward Beecher, who became a nationally known clergyman, received $450 a year at his first church after graduation from seminary in Cincinnati—the First Presbyterian Church of Aurora, which had a congregation of twenty, of which nineteen were women.

The study of White House china for its role in history was started by first lady Caroline Harrison of Indiana, who designed the china she and her husband Benjamin Harrison used during his presidency. The china bore the U.S. coat of arms surrounded by a wide, dark-blue border etched in gold and including designs of goldenrod and corn. It was made in France.

Indiana passed a law in 1970 permitting falconry in the state for the first time; a registered falconer was permitted two hawks for pursuing game.

Avoca in Lawrence County was named for a poem: "Sweet vale of Avoca, how calm could I rest / In the bosom of thy shade, with the friend I love best." It was a favorite of Doctor Winthrop Foote, a pioneer who often read poetry in the area where Avoca was platted in 1819.

One of the largest Ku Klux Klan conventions in the nation was held on July 4, 1923, at Kokomo, attracting more than one hundred thousand Klansmen from as far away as Florida and California. A similar event on July 4, 1924, was almost as successful and included a parade featuring the Kokomo Klan's thirty-three-piece band.

Sharon Dereamer of Hancock County became the first woman inducted into the Rotary Club of Indiana when she joined the Greenfield Rotary Club on June 16, 1987.

Early in the 1900s decks of playing cards were printed using Indiana authors as a theme; James Whitcomb Riley appeared on all the deuces in the decks. Other authors used were Edward Eggleston, Booth Tarkington, Maurice Thompson, and poet Evaleen Stein.

The statue on the Bedford courthouse square is unusual because it was erected relatively late, 1924; pays tribute not only to veterans, but also pioneers; has a face in the likeness of Bedford resident Mayme Hubbard Smith; and is said to contain a crypt concealing excerpts from a book, a will, and military rosters. The book, *Diary of a Lawyer*, and the will are said to be those of Bedford attorney Moses F. Dunn, whose bequest in 1915 sparked the plan for the statue. However, so far nobody has been able to locate the crypt.

Peru's extensive collection of circus memorabilia, which was assembled in tribute to that town's role as headquarters for circuses in winter, acquired a massive addition in 1985. A price of $425,000 was paid to John and Jan Zwiefel of Orlando, Florida, for their collection of twenty-four circus wagons, a library, costumes, and props from early circus days.

Education

Andrew Crawford, Azel W. Dorsey, and James Sweeney were the three schoolmasters who tutored Abraham Lincoln during the time he went to formal school in Indiana, about a year, starting in 1818.

Baynard Rush Hall, the first teacher at the state seminary, later Indiana University, earned $250 a year to teach Greek and Latin and earned extra income by preaching in the Presbyterian church.

Before a change in 1891 that shortened commencement exercises at Indiana University in Bloomington, each graduate gave a speech at commencement. Guests often took picnic lunches to the long ceremonies.

Merom in Sullivan County is said to be the smallest town in the United States to be the site of a Carnegie Library, acquired at the behest of J. J. Parker, operator of the Merom drugstore, in the 1930s.

Edward Rector, who created an extensive scholarship fund at DePauw University, graduated from high school in Bedford at the age of fourteen but never attended college because of the lack of money.

The library at Linton was built in 1908–9 with funds from the Carnegie Foundation. But the name Carnegie was not used for the library because it was feared

Carnegie Library, Merom.

that mine laborers and their families might not use a facility honoring the name of an industrialist.

Vincennes University, which was chartered by the first General Assembly of the Indiana Territory and completed its first building in 1811, is the oldest comprehensive junior college in the United States. Its charter provides for free board, clothes, and education for Indian students.

Among developments at New Harmony were the nation's first infant school, the first trade school, the first public school where boys and girls received equal education, the first civic dramatic club, and the first headquarters of the U.S. Geological Survey.

The first yearlong school to train librarians in Indiana was founded by Merica Evans Hoagland in 1905 in Indianapolis, but the school became the subject of controversy over funding and legislative support and closed in 1912.

Poet Ezra Pound was hired for one year as professor of romance languages at Wabash College in 1907 but was fired after three months when his landlady found a burlesque queen in his room. Nobody knows how a burlesque queen got in his room or got in Crawfordsville, which Pound called Devil's Island, Indiana.

When noted humorist Don Herold of Bloomfield became president of the Indiana University Alumni Association in 1943, he proposed the creation in the university of a Chair of Levity. Whether he got a laugh seems unrecorded.

Chicago gangster Al Capone enrolled in a science course of study at the University of Notre Dame in 1937, later changing to commerce. He left in 1938 due to "poor scholarship." Capone's nephew, Ralph Gabriel Capone, also attended one semester at Notre Dame in 1935.

Lillian Moller Gilbreth's appointment in 1935 at Purdue University marked the hiring of the first woman professor of management employed at any university in America. She was the widow of Frank Gilbreth, expert on time studies, the subject of the book *Cheaper by the Dozen.*

The Department of English at Purdue University offered Thomas Wolfe, who stuttered, $300 to speak at the group's annual literary banquet on May 19, 1938. Four months later Wolfe, whose talk was a big success, died in Baltimore after becoming ill with pneumonia.

Valparaiso University was once sold to the Ku Klux Klan and the sale was publicly announced, but the deal fell through. In 1925 the Lutheran University Association acquired the college.

The Valparaiso University Chapel of the Resurrection, largest college chapel in the world, can seat three thousand people.

Southern Indiana Normal College, founded at Mitchell in 1880, was nicknamed SIN College, but it often had a larger enrollment than Indiana University—nine hundred students when it burned in 1900.

Thomas Marshall, later U.S. vice president, was sued for $20,000 while a senior at Wabash College on charges of libeling a female lecturer in a student newspaper article. The suit was filed by Lew Wallace, later famous as a novelist, among other things. Marshall and other students were defended for free by Benjamin Harrison, later U.S. president, who extricated them from the suit.

The Hebron public library, dedicated in 1922, is believed to have been the last of 149 libraries built in Indiana with the help of the Carnegie Foundation.

The William A. Wirt education plan in Gary, begun in 1910, was copied by more than a thousand schools in 202 cities before it was replaced in many places by other education theories after his death in 1938. His plan created platoons of students who changed classes for different subjects, increasing the number of students a school could handle.

The Louis A. Warren Lincoln Library and Museum at Fort Wayne has more than three hundred documents signed by Abraham Lincoln.

John Snedeker of Muncie presented degrees to three of his sons at the same time in 1976 at Western New Mexico University, of which he was president. Patrick and Philip, twins, completed college in three years so as to be graduated with their brother John, who was eleven months older.

The first graduating class of Wabash College in 1838 consisted of Archibald C. Allen and Silas Jessup.

The real name of the New Harmony teacher known as William S. Phiquepal was Guillaume Sylvan Casimir Phiquepal d'Arusmont. A member of Robert Owen's "Boatload of Knowledge" that arrived in New Harmony in 1826, Phiquepal was an advocate of Johann Heinrich Pestalozzi, a Swiss reformer in education.

The Indiana School for the Blind once had a roller skating rink. The area later was turned into a student center. However, skating still was done on sidewalks around the school on the north side of Indianapolis.

When William Willard opened a school for the deaf in Indianapolis in 1843, which later became the Indiana School for the Deaf, he was the first deaf man in America to start a permanent school for the nonhearing.

Samuel A. Elbert, after first being refused a degree from Indiana Medical College, finally got the degree in 1871 and became the first African American in Indiana to receive one.

Saint Mary-of-the-Woods near Terre Haute is the oldest Catholic women's college in the United States; Saint Mary's College at South Bend is the second oldest.

Manchester College, which started out as Roanoke Classic Seminary in 1861 at Roanoke, Indiana, later was owned by the United Brethren Conference before becoming the property of D. N. Howe, who moved it to North Manchester.

The first consolidated school in Indiana was Raleigh School in northeast Rush County, which opened in 1877 to bring in students from five one-room schoolhouses. It closed in 1968 when Rush County elementary and secondary schools were consolidated.

A commencement speech by Wendell Willkie at Indiana University in 1916 was termed by IU president William Lowe Bryan the "most radical speech he ever had heard." Willkie criticized the law faculty for its conservatism and rapped the state constitution. Willkie's diploma was withheld for two days until the dean of the School of Law could reprimand Willkie, the law school's top student.

Robert Dale Owen, whose father purchased New Harmony, was born in Scotland but was educated in Switzerland at Hofwyl near Bern.

Andrew Wylie, first president of Indiana University and a strong believer in manual labor, cut his foot while chopping wood, his favorite labor, and died as a result. He was unable to return home on his own and lay in the woods until found by passersby. His exposure, a return to presidential duties too soon, and the development of pneumonia brought his death in 1851 at the age of sixty-two.

When Ray Vagus, twenty-eight years old, got a four-year degree in absentia from Ball State University in May 1981, he was the first prison inmate in Indiana to do so. He was serving a fifteen- to twenty-five-year sentence for second degree murder. His degree was in—what else?—criminal justice. Jon Taylor earned a bachelor's degree in history from Ball State University in 1989 by taking courses during his eighteen years in the Indiana Reformatory.

Liber College, founded in 1835 at Portland, had a school ballad including these lines: "They will teach you how to read and write, / Arithmetic they'll teach you, / So that no cunning rascal might / In trading overreach you."

The first campus Young Men's Christian Association in the world was formed in 1870 at Hanover College, where a special building to house it was constructed in 1883 and survived more than a century.

Angola High School in 1991 was the first high school in Indiana linked to the Ball State University online public access catalog, a computer database of 1.4 million volumes in the Ball State library.

Mike Uslan taught the first college course in comic books at Indiana University in Bloomington in 1971 and 1972. Uslan, an undergraduate history major, taught J213 for three semesters. Later he studied law and went into the movie business.

Purdue University was founded in 1869 at Chauncey, a town which had been named only three years earlier; the town was merged with Kingston to become West Lafayette in 1888.

The Purdue University seal, adopted in 1928, replaced one that had been used for seventy-three years but never was officially approved by the board of trustees. The official seal was designed by Professor Al Bowan.

The Tippecanoe County morgue was moved into Lynn Hall on the Purdue University campus in 1975.

When Purdue University tried to thwart the school's first fraternity—the underground Delta chapter of Sigma Chi—it resulted in a court battle that reached the Indiana Supreme Court in 1882. The highest Indiana court ruled that membership in the fraternity was "no impropriety," and faculty objection to it or "other fraternities of the same class was unfounded." The ruling set a precedent for fraternities in colleges everywhere.

Stories that the body of John Purdue has been dug up by students from his grave on the Purdue University campus is not supported by any evidence.

A total of nineteen graduates of Purdue University have served as presidents or chancellors of institutes of higher learning—including Arthur G. Hansen, class of 1946, who was president of Purdue University from 1970 to 1981 and was the first alumnus to hold that post.

In 1966 Sylvia Butler of Angola won a high-school speaking contest as part of the Indiana Sesquicentennial.

George Ade's first published work was a high school theme called "A Basket of Potatoes," which his teacher submitted to the Kentland newspaper in 1881. Ade pointed out how large potatoes could be shaken to the top of a basket and offered suggestions on how to become a big potato through study and good character.

When Paul V. McNutt, later to be governor of Indiana, was appointed dean of the IU Law School he became the youngest dean of any accredited law school in the nation at the age of thirty-four.

Yale University once owned ten square miles of Benton County. It was bequeathed to the university by Hoosier Henry L. Ellsworth, commissioner of U.S. patents, who strongly believed in the richness of unbroken prairie soil. Ellsworth gave Yale about five thousand acres in other counties too.

Saint Joseph's Indian Normal School, founded in 1888 at Collegeville near Rensselaer, had problems with students coming from far-off tribal locations and running away due to homesickness. Truancy was such a problem that only six of the first class of fifty completed the five-year educational program.

Marjorie A. Woodruff taught for forty-four years in Public School 44 in Indianapolis and was mentioned for it in Ripley's *Believe It or Not* in 1986, when she was eighty-five years old, well after her retirement in 1967.

Events

According to George Ade, when he decided to have a picnic for children at his estate of Hazelden near Brook about 1910, he sent out five hundred invitations and received eight hundred acceptances. Attendance reached two thousand annually before Ade discontinued the picnics in about 1930.

The first known public plea for a national day honoring mothers was made on Monument Circle in Indianapolis on February 7, 1904, by Frank E. Hering, addressing members of the Fraternal Order of Eagles; the site was the old English Hotel and Opera House.

Rudolph M. Crandall, a ham radio operator living at Richmond, sent a message on January 3, 1931, which was relayed via other operators around the world and back to Richmond in thirty-seven minutes, a historic event at the time.

The *South Bend Tribune* established the first successful radio station in Indiana with a hundred-watt transmitter in a third-floor auditorium in July 1922.

When a car driven by Charles H. Black, its inventor, frightened a horse on an Indianapolis street in the 1890s, the damages—a strap broken on the wagon the steed was pulling—cost Black one dollar. It may have been the least expensive auto accident of all time.

The first Thanksgiving Day was proclaimed in Indiana in March 1822 by Jonathan Jennings, the first governor, who set aside the second Friday in April to give thanks for the state coming through a devastating statewide bout of illness. The first official Thanksgiving Day was proclaimed for November 28, 1839, by Governor David Wallace, who urged prayers of thanks for "our civil and religious liberty." This was twenty-five years before Thanksgiving became a national holiday in 1864.

The recipe for turtle soup, served for years at an annual festival at Ferdinand, was so secret that it was kept in a safe deposit box in the Dubois County Bank and taken out only when it came time to make the soup.

In one of the most bizarre cases in railroad history, the famed Toledo-St. Louis train, called the Commercial Traveler, was hit by a tornado about 11 a.m. on March 21, 1916, near Hanfield in Grant County. The twister blew all the train cars off the track, leaving the engine untouched, and depositing cars twenty feet away on their sides. Yet no one was killed and only five people required hospitalization. The engineer and fireman, both untouched, drove the unharmed engine to nearby Marion and hauled doctors to the scene.

When a nine-foot stone obelisk was dedicated near the village of Millhousen in 1891 to mark the United States' center of population, the event attracted a crowd of more than ten thousand.

1890 Center of Population Marker.

THE INDIANA BOOK OF TRIVIA

In 1992 Steve Carter of Plainfield rode a high-wheeled bicycle 3,428 miles coast to coast in thirty-three days and seven hours, a world record.

The first mail delivery to Indianapolis was made in April 1822, by Lewis Jones, who came to the capital on horseback from the Connersville post office.

Crusader Carrie Nation appeared in Crawfordsville in 1901 as a Fourth of July orator sponsored by the Elks, who cleared five hundred dollars in the fund-raiser from a crowd estimated at eight thousand. Nation sold pictures, toy hatchets (her symbol for breaking up saloons as a temperance fighter), and *The Smasher's Mail*, her newsletter.

The Feast of the Hunters' Moon at Lafayette marks the fact that Fort Ouiatenon was the first permanent European settlement in Indiana, established in 1717. The true site of the fort is in question, but it is believed to have been near the confluence of Wea Creek and the Wabash River.

At Ridgeville in Randolph County, an annual June festival created an unusual town landmark, a circle of numbers painted on the pavement in the town square. It was used in a feature of the celebration staged by the American Legion Auxiliary—a cakewalk.

The famed Daniel Webster made a Fourth of July speech at Michigan City in 1837, proving his oratorical ability could be affected by drink. After being wined and dined, he began a speech on the national debt by saying "The national debt." Pausing to put his hands in his pockets, he finally continued, "how much is the damned thing?"

The 1860 census showed Indiana had ten hogs for every family. The number of "pork barrels" was not recorded.

Flooding in 1882–84 left Evansville dry on high ground. From there Clara Barton launched the first Red Cross flood relief program.

When rural free delivery was started at Hope in 1896, it was not only the first RFD in Indiana, it also was the second in the nation. Albert Hitchcock made deliveries by horse and buggy.

The *Robert E. Lee* steamboat, built at Jeffersonville, won a race from New Orleans to Saint Louis against the *Natchez* in 1870 in three and three-quarter days, a record that still stands.

The first Indiana State Fair ran for five days in October 1852 and brought in $14,600 through an admission price of twenty cents per person.

Although the first Indiana State Fair was held in Indianapolis in 1852, as it is now, the fair was held at Lafayette in 1853, Madison in 1854, New Albany in 1859, Fort Wayne in 1865, and Terre Haute in 1867.

In 1931 during the Indiana State Fair, sixteen tons of manure were stolen, according to fair officials, who seemingly never were able to put authorities on the scent of the culprits.

Lotteries are not new in Indiana. In 1807 Vincennes University, just granted a charter, was authorized to raise money for equipment with a lottery. There also was a lottery in 1818 to raise money for a canal around the falls of the Ohio River at Louisville and a lottery in 1825 in Hamilton County to raise money for a new courthouse. Both these latter lotteries failed.

The last time former U.S. vice president Thomas R. Marshall was in Indiana was 1925 when he gave a commencement address at his hometown, North Manchester (for the college there). He died ten days later.

Famed orator William Jennings Bryan, addressing the Island Park Assembly Chautauqua in Noble County in 1910, got only $110.55 for his share of the receipts and was accused of stealing the valise containing the rest of the gate. He denied it, vowed never to visit there again, and never did.

The steamboat *Argosy III* was caught in a storm near Magnet in Perry County, and ten Civil War veterans going home to Cincinnati drowned when the boat's boiler exploded, forcing them overboard. Local farmers and survivors buried the dead in a mass grave. The incident did not come to light until 1962. The U.S. government erected ten white stone markers in memorial at the site in 1965.

Thomas R. Marshall birthplace.

Fred Cavinder

Cannelton was the only Hoosier city defended by naval gunboats during the Civil War, a measure taken to protect the Indiana cotton mill's production of cotton goods used by the Union troops. Confederate renegades had threatened to burn the mill.

The first train to enter the tunnel built in 1877 by the Ohio and Mississippi Railroad near Tunnelton (named for the tunnel) stalled and was pulled out by mules.

Government and Politics

The Indiana General Assembly, meeting in Corydon soon after statehood, not only banned wagers in Indiana but also decreed that if two persons bet, both the winner and loser should be fined double the amount won or lost.

From 1818 to 1825 the oath of office taken by the Indiana governor required that official, and also other state officials, to swear "not to participate in duels or allow others to participate." Duels were conducted in Indiana from 1809, when it was a territory, to the 1850s when the last known duels were fought—but not, as far as is known, by governors.

Although she became First Lady with the 1840 election of her husband, William Henry Harrison, as president, Anna Symmes Harrison never occupied the White House. She had not left the Harrison home in North Bend, Ohio, before she learned that Harrison, former governor of the Indiana Territory, had died in Washington one month after being sworn in as president, at sixty-eight years of age. Harrison held the record as the oldest man elected to that office until 1980 when Ronald Reagan was elected.

William Henry Harrison and Anna Symmes eloped late in 1795 because Anna's father, John Cleves Symmes, former chief justice of the New Jersey Supreme Court, refused to agree to his daughter marrying Harrison, then a young soldier.

A bill in the Indiana General Assembly to change the mathematical value of pi, used to measure circles, from 3.1416 to 3.2 was introduced on January 18, 1897, by state representative Taylor I. Record, a Posey County farmer. The bill was eventually postponed on the motion of state senator Orrin Z. Hubbell of Elkhart, thus saving the state from international mathematical embarrassment. Go figure.

The first organized movement in Indiana to give women equal rights began at a convention in 1851 in the United Brethren Church in Dublin, where the main address was given by Doctor Mary F. Thomas, a noted physician in Richmond and the first female member of the state medical society. She presented a petition for women's suffrage to the Indiana General Assembly in 1859. The legislature turned down the request.

Judge Stephen Neal of Lebanon wrote the Fourteenth Amendment to the U.S. Constitution, which granted citizenship to African Americans, in 1866. Neal, who came to Lebanon in 1843, had been an Indiana legislator from 1846 to 1847. He sent his version of the amendment to Godlove S. Orth, a former fellow state legislator and then a congressman from the Ninth District. Orth gave it to the fifteen-man committee in Congress, which approved the amendment, adding a fifth section to the four Neal had written.

Ira Joy Chase enlisted in Illinois as a sergeant in the Civil War and was wounded and hospitalized at Nashville, Tennessee. His wife Rhoda Chase went to Nashville and became an army nurse in order to tend her husband and other soldiers. She contracted smallpox, which blinded her. Ira became a Disciples of Christ minister and served congregations at Mishawaka, La Porte, Danville, and Wabash before he was elected lieutenant governor in 1888. Chase became the twenty-first governor of Indiana on the death of Alvin Hovey in 1891, making his wife, blind for sixty years, the First Lady of Indiana.

Ira J. Chase, while governor of Indiana in 1891–93, lived in Danville and commuted daily to the statehouse by train.

Ira J. Chase, elected and elevated to governor, was a man who never before had held public office.

Records are inexact, but evidence is that Indiana became the twentieth state to require drivers' licenses in 1921. Driving tests, physical exams, and eye tests began in late 1937, written tests in 1945.

On December 12, 1816, the day after Indiana was admitted to the Union, two senators chosen by the Indiana General Assembly drew lots. Senator James Noble drew first and got the longer term—to March 3, 1821. Senator Waller Taylor got the shorter term—until March 3, 1819. Noble was reelected twice and died in office. Taylor was reelected once.

Henry Dodge of Vincennes, after a distinguished career in the military during the War of 1812 and the Blackhawk War, served in the U.S. Senate at the same time as his son, Caesar Augustus Dodge, also served as a senator from Iowa.

In 1892 in Nappanee all four of the political parties in town offering candidates for four trustee posts, clerk, treasurer, and marshal failed to file a list of candidates with the county clerk fifteen days before the election as required by law, so the voting was a scoreless tie. The incumbents automatically succeeded themselves, and nobody seemed to mind very much.

The first women in the Indiana General Assembly were Julia D. Nelson of Delaware County, appointed to the House of Representatives to replace Clark D.

McKinley, a candidate who died three days before the election in 1920, and Arcada Stark Balz of Marion County, elected a senator in 1942 to represent Marion and Johnson counties.

James S. Hinton was the first African American elected to the Indiana General Assembly in 1880, running as a Republican. He had served in the Civil War as a recruiter for black troops and attended the GOP national convention in 1872. He was a barber and active in the black Masons in Indiana and the African Methodist Episcopal Church. He died in 1892 in Brazil, Indiana.

Joseph Lane of Vanderburgh County was commissioned governor of the Oregon Territory, later served as a U.S. senator from Oregon, and was nominated for vice president with John C. Breckinridge in 1860. When defeated in a smear campaign, he returned to his Indiana farm, then near Roseburg in Union County, and died there.

Ann Delaney was the first woman in Indiana to run (unsuccessfully) for lieutenant governor, as a Democratic candidate in 1983 with running mate Wayne Townsend.

When President and Mrs. Benjamin Harrison moved into the White House, they brought along a family of eleven: a son and daughter, their spouses, and three children; Mrs. Harrison's eighty-nine-year-old father; and her widowed niece. At that time, 1889, the White House had one bathroom. In later years Harrison said, "There has never been an hour since I left the White House that I have felt a wish to return to it." Draw your own conclusion.

Benjamin Harrison was elected over Grover Cleveland for the U.S. presidency in 1888 while getting only 47.9 percent of the popular vote; Cleveland got 48.6 percent. The 1892 election saw Cleveland win with only 46.1 percent, while Harrison received only 43 percent.

Three Hoosiers have directed the U.S. State Department—John M. Hay of Salem, John W. Foster of Pike County, and Walter Q. Gresham of Lanesville.

A major supporter of Eugene V. Debs of Terre Haute in his campaigns for the presidency as a socialist was Helen Keller, an avid socialist and communist supporter.

When Debs ran for president while imprisoned for violating the Sedition Act of 1918, his prison number at Atlanta, Georgia, was 9653.

Before being elected Indiana governor and later U.S. vice president, Thomas R. Marshall, practicing law at Columbia City, became an alcoholic, drinking so much he sometimes appeared in court intoxicated. He took the "cure" in 1898 and soon was deeply (and successfully) involved in Democrat politics.

When Thomas R. Marshall of Whitley County stood in place of Woodrow Wilson while the president was in Europe at the World War I peace conference, it was the first time a vice president presided over cabinet meetings.

Vice President Thomas R. Marshall twice refused to join ploys to elevate him to president over Woodrow Wilson—once when Wilson went to France (the Republicans claimed he had abdicated his office) and once when Wilson became ill in 1919 (power brokers claimed he was incapable of performing his duties).

Republican U.S. senator Harry S. New, running for reelection in 1922, was the first to use radio extensively in Indiana in the campaign against Democrat Samuel Moffett Ralston, who defeated him.

F. Harold Van Orman, who served as state senator from Evansville and as lieutenant governor in the administration of Governor Ed Jackson, is said to have coined the phrase "Indiana has the best legislature money can buy."

Roberta West Nicholson, who served in the Indiana General Assembly in the 1935 session, was noted in headlines around the globe for her bill that made it illegal for Indiana women to sue men for breach of promise. This "anti-heart balm" legislation was passed and was copied by eleven other states.

Harold W. Handley was one of the few Indiana governors elected in modern times who was not a lawyer. He was in office from 1957 to 1961.

Indiana congressman Charles A. Halleck of Rensselaer was promised a chance to be Thomas E. Dewey's running mate in 1948 in exchange for delivering nomination votes to Dewey. Dewey, however, reneged; Dewey also lost the election to Harry S Truman.

"Keep the ball rolling" is an expression stemming from the presidential campaign of William Henry Harrison, Indiana's first territorial governor. The motto was one of many written on a six-foot paper ball that his supporters rolled from town to town. Later, to gain publicity, a ball twice a man's height was rolled from Maryland along the National Road to the Indianapolis home of Benjamin Harrison as part of his 1888 presidential election campaign. The phrase apparently was adopted from the British, who applied it to ballgames in the eighteenth century.

A total of twenty-seven Hoosiers, native or adopted, ran for U.S. president or vice president in twenty-two consecutive elections from 1836 to 1940.

William Bercik, his wife Mary, and their son Robert J. all served as mayor of Whiting. Mary, elected in 1960, was the first female to be elected mayor in Indiana.

Wendell Lewis Willkie, unsuccessful Republican presidential candidate in 1940 from Elwood, was named Lewis Wendell Willkie. But he said that in World War I the army got it backwards. He gave up trying to correct it and became known thenceforth as Wendell L. Willkie.

Fred Cavinder

Mary Bercik.

Wendell L. Willkie adopted Rushville as his home and ran his presidential campaign from there because Rushville was the birthplace of his wife Edith.

When Wendell Willkie ran for president in 1940, the Republicans had a campaign song, written by R. W. White, titled "We Want Willkie."

Wendell Willkie, traveling around the world as an emissary for President Franklin D. Roosevelt, who had beaten Willkie for the presidency in 1940, carried letters of introduction to world leaders. He lost some of the letters, including the one to Stalin, which was eventually found and put in the Library of Congress.

On June 19, 1950, Paul D. Abbott entered a six-by-six-by-sixteen foot furnished chamber under Lake Schafer's water to protest an excise tax. He came out August 6, 1950, without having produced any effect on the tax.

When Democrat Richard Corns was elected mayor of Elkhart in 1959 and a recount gave the vote to his opponent, Frank Parmater, by a few votes, the recount also was contested. After delays and confusion, it was agreed that Parmater would serve as mayor for 1960–61 and Corns would serve as controller during that time, and then they would trade jobs for the last two years of the term of office.

The first speech of William Howard Taft in his GOP presidential campaign tour in 1908 was given at Hazelden, the Brook, Indiana, home of author George Ade.

Samuel L. Shank, controversial Indianapolis mayor from 1910 to 1913, resigned from office four weeks early to go on the vaudeville circuit in Kansas City and New York to talk about his mayoral term. As mayor he had auctioned off vegetables on the steps of city hall, crusaded against saloons being open on Sunday, and survived a 1913 streetcar strike that involved a mutiny by police who refused to protect strikebreakers manning the streetcars.

The first Hoosier to serve in a presidential cabinet was Caleb B. Smith, a Bostonian who came to Connersville in 1827 to study law. Smith became a newspaper editor, was a state legislator and U.S. congressman, and served as President Abraham Lincoln's secretary of interior (1861–63).

John W. Foster of Pike County, then former U.S. Secretary of State, was called upon in 1894 to negotiate peace between Japan and China, which the Japanese had conquered. He was so successful that he received China's highest award, the Order of the Golden Grain.

Because of his heroic action at Fort Harrison near Terre Haute in 1811, Zachary Taylor was recommended for promotion to brevet major by territorial governor William Henry Harrison. It began an impressive career that led Taylor to the U.S. presidency in 1849—nine years after Harrison himself was elected president. Both men died in office, the only presidents to die in the executive mansion.

Frank Beckwith, an Indianapolis attorney who ran for president in the primary elections in 1960 and 1964 and was the first African American to do so, did not formally attend law school, but was tutored by the dean of a law school and passed the bar exam. He had tried to enter the all-white Benjamin Harrison Law School in Indianapolis and had been told he could enter the school if all the class members approved. One disapproved, which blackballed Beckwith. Beckwith received twenty thousand votes in each of the primary elections.

The first African American to serve on a grand jury in Indiana was James T. V. Hill, who came to Indianapolis from Ohio in 1874 and became an attorney. He served on the Indianapolis grand jury in 1890.

In 1987 Osma Spurlock became not only the first woman, but also the first African American appointed director of a federal agency in the state when named to head the Equal Employment Opportunity Commission in Indiana and Kentucky.

General John Tipton gave thirty acres of his holdings in Bartholomew County for a county seat, providing it would be named to honor him. When the county commissioners named it Columbus instead, Tipton left and settled in northern Indiana.

Claude Bowers, after his graduation from Indianapolis High School (later renamed Shortridge High School) in January 1898, won the state high school oratorical contest in March at Richmond in an era when such ability provided high status before the advent of basketball. He was later U.S. ambassador to Spain and Chile.

Ralph F. Gates, governor of Indiana from 1945 to 1949, was the paperboy who delivered the paper in Columbia City to Thomas R. Marshall, who had been Indiana governor from 1909 to 1913 and U.S. vice president from 1913 to 1921.

John Hay, who was born in Salem and who was a statesman, diplomat, poet, historian, secretary to President Abraham Lincoln, secretary of state under President William McKinley, and ambassador to Britain, greatly disliked Indiana and considered himself a "man without a state."

John Hay was at the bedsides of Abraham Lincoln, William McKinley, and James Garfield when each died as a result of assassin bullets. They all had been U.S. presidents whom Hay had served.

Christopher Harrison of Maryland was a recluse living near the site of Hanover College in 1808, allegedly a self-imposed exile because of a broken love affair. In 1815 he abandoned his hermit existence, opened a store with a partner in Salem, Indiana, and in 1816 was elected Indiana lieutenant governor. In 1818 he resigned in a dispute over Governor Jonathan Jennings accepting a federal post.

Richard Hatcher of Gary and Carl Stokes of Cleveland became the first African American mayors of major northern cities with their elections in 1967.

In 1849 Samuel Henderson, first mayor of Indianapolis, left town and headed west because he didn't think the Indiana capital would ever amount to much.

In 1831 Indiana adopted legislation requiring African Americans moving into the state to post a five-hundred-dollar bond as a promise of "good behavior" and a guarantee against becoming a public charge.

A constitutional amendment calling for a referendum of voters before war can be declared was proposed by Louis Ludlow of Indiana, but a vote of 209 to 188 in Congress shelved the proposal in 1938.

Katie Beatrice Hall of Gary not only was the first African American woman from Indiana elected to Congress (1982–85), she also introduced the bill making the birthday of Martin Luther King Jr. a federal holiday.

The man considered pivotal in getting Benjamin Harrison elected president in 1888 was Louis Michener of Connersville, an attorney in Shelbyville, a close friend of Harrison, and once Indiana attorney general. Declining a post in the Harrison administration, Michener moved his law practice to Washington, D.C., and was a frequent visitor to the White House. He managed Harrison's renomination drive through a secret letter-writing campaign to GOP leaders across the country. Harrison was renominated but lost to Grover Cleveland.

The wife of notorious Louisiana politician Huey Long, who was assassinated, was Rose McConnell, born in Greensburg. She succeeded her husband in the U.S. Senate, becoming the first female senator from Louisiana.

Four Hoosiers became governors of western states: J. P. St. John, governor of Kansas; Henry G. Blaisdell, governor of Nevada; Newton Booth, governor of California; and Ernest M. Cooper, governor of the Hawaiian Islands. (Cooper served briefly as president of the Republic of Hawaii before it was annexed to the United States.)

After serving as Indiana governor, James P. Goodrich traveled to Russia four times in 1921, 1922, and 1925 to investigate the great famine there. As a result, he became an advocate of trade with the USSR, an unpopular stand at the time.

Every county in Indiana has had at least two county courthouses. Some have had as many as five, a few even more.

Indiana's first female county court judge was Linda Chezem, appointed in Lawrence County on January 1, 1976.

Indiana banned smoking in a bill passed in 1905 that was amended twice but not lifted completely until 1977.

Two men from landlocked Indiana served as U.S. secretaries of the navy—Richard W. Thompson of Bedford (1877–80) and Edwin Denby of Evansville (1921–24).

The practice of public hangings in Indiana was halted due to the circus atmosphere surrounding the 1886 execution of Nathaniel S. Bates at Richmond for killing his estranged wife Catherine. A bill was passed in 1889 requiring executions to be conducted at the state penitentiary. Wayne County sheriff Isaac Alex Gorman, who sprang the trapdoor to hang Bates, led the drive for revision of the hanging law.

Tecumseh and Suwarrow were two of several names suggested for the Indiana capital until the 1821 Indiana General Assembly, meeting at Corydon, chose Indianapolis.

Mainly because of his talent as a lecturer, Hoosier poet James Whitcomb Riley for twenty-five years was a guest at the White House of each succeeding U.S. president.

Indiana's U.S. senator Jesse D. Bright of Madison was asked to be secretary of state by President James Buchanan, but declined.

Senator Jesse D. Bright opposed the Civil War because he held slaves at his Kentucky farm. With the war imminent, he gave a letter of introduction to Confederate president Jefferson Davis recommending Thomas Lincoln of Texas as a firearms salesman. The letter caused Bright's expulsion from the U.S. Senate.

In an effort to bring some uniformity to the spelling of cities and towns in the United States, President Benjamin Harrison of Indianapolis created the U.S. Board of Geographic Names in 1890.

Virginia E. Jenckes of Terre Haute, elected in 1932 as the first woman in Congress from Indiana, battled against communism during three terms and charged that Russia had offered her $200,000 and a free trip to that country if she would stop her attacks.

As president pro tem of the Indiana State Senate, James Brown Ray became Indiana governor because both the governor, William Hendricks, and the lieutenant governor, Ratliff Boon, had resigned to seek or assume U.S. congressional posts.

James Brown Ray of Brookville ruined his career as Indiana governor because he backed railroad expansion over canal system expansion—not until later did his

James Ray Brown home, Brookville.

prediction of a rail network come to be. Earlier he had to win election as governor in 1825 over charges that the Palladian window in his Brookville home was a mark of extravagance ill-becoming the head of state.

Crown Hill Cemetery in Indianapolis has the graves of three vice presidents of the United States: Thomas A. Hendricks, Thomas R. Marshall, and Charles W. Fairbanks, and the graves of three who ran for that office unsuccessfully, George W. Julian, William H. English, and John W. Kern.

Only eight of the ninety-two Indiana counties have courthouses less than fifty years old; all but five of the courthouses are on town squares.

William D. McCarty, a senator in the Indiana General Assembly from Anderson in the 1990s, was interested in vampires and served as unofficial president of the Indiana Fan Club for Dracula.

In 1923 Thomas Taggart, politician and political power broker in Indianapolis and elsewhere in the state, invited the entire Indiana General Assembly and reporters covering the session to the French Lick Springs Hotel, which he owned.

Nine counties—the record number during any year—were formed in Indiana in 1818; in 1836 seven counties were formed.

Indiana, founded in 1816, did not have a statewide primary election until March 7, 1916, when Charles W. Fairbanks of Indianapolis was a candidate for U.S. president. In the first statewide primary election voters could select their first and second choices of nominees for office.

Although five Hoosiers were elected vice president of the United States from Indiana, only two were actually born in the state—Dan Quayle and Thomas R. Marshall. In all, nine Hoosiers have been nominated for the vice presidency.

Two former Hoosier governors had the shortest terms as U.S. president and vice president. President William Henry Harrison died in 1841 after only a month in office, and Thomas Hendricks lived only nine months as vice president under Grover Cleveland, dying in March 1885.

Ron Schenkel, while mayor of Huntington, claimed to have visited every Indiana town with a population of five thousand or more, a total of 115. He said he was looking for civic examples that might work for Huntington. His last stop was New Albany.

Four Hoosiers have served as U.S. postmasters general—James N. Tyner of Brookville, Walter Q. Gresham of Harrison County, Will H. Hays of Sullivan, and Harry S. New of Indianapolis.

Thomas Taggart.

Richard G. Lugar and Theodore F. Stevens both attended School 84 in Indianapolis and both ended up in the U.S. Senate—Lugar from Indiana in the 1990s and Stevens from Alaska, elected in 1968. Stevens attended the school eight years ahead of Lugar.

When Charles W. Fairbanks of Indianapolis and Thomas R. Marshall of North Manchester ran for vice president in 1916—Fairbanks with Charles Evans Hughes and Marshall with Woodrow Wilson—it was the first time in history both vice presidential candidates were from the same state.

William Henry Harrison and his grandson Benjamin Harrison, both president of the United States, both died of pneumonia, William thirty days after his 1841 inauguration and Benjamin in 1901, eight years after leaving the White House.

Joseph Chapman, a Greenfield orator and saloon owner, "crowed" so much about his Democratic Party in the 1840 presidential campaign that the rooster became the party symbol.

The Barnett-Seawright-Wilson house in Delphi is where President Franklin D. Roosevelt once had tea with Henry B. Wilson, prominent Democrat and newspaperman, when Wilson owned the house.

When Horace Greeley, New York newspaper editor, ran for U.S. president in 1872, losing to Ulysses S. Grant, he died before the Electoral College could meet—the only time this has happened. Unable to vote for Greeley, forty-two of the sixty-six Indiana electors voted for Thomas A. Hendricks, ex-governor of Indiana, as a favorite-son gesture. Grant got the office, however.

Famed trial lawyer Clarence Darrow gave the eulogy in 1921 for Thomas Knotts, elected the first mayor of Gary in 1909. Knotts was fluent in the language of the Sioux. When Knotts lost his reelection bid as a Democrat in 1913, another Democrat was not elected Gary mayor until 1935.

Oliver P. Morton, probably best known for his support of Abraham Lincoln and for borrowing money to run the state when the legislature walked out during the Civil War, was the first native of Indiana to serve as governor.

The shortest term for an Indiana governor was that of Henry S. Lane; inaugurated January 14, 1861, he resigned on January 16 to accept an appointment to the U.S. Senate.

Joseph A. Wright was elected Indiana governor for three years in 1849 under the old constitution; in 1852 he was reelected for a four-year term under the new state constitution.

Three governors in a row came from Brookville, where they had made their homes upon coming to Indiana: James Brown Ray, Noah Noble, and David Wallace. They served between 1825 and 1840.

Indiana's first elected governor, Jonathan Jennings, who served two three-year terms, was a native of New Jersey.

The second governor of the Indiana Territory, John Gibson, once was captured by Cayuga Indians and was to die at the stake until an old squaw rescued him and adopted him. Gibson was acting territorial governor for nearly two years.

Governor James A. Mount, who lobbied to gain passage of Indiana's first compulsory education law in 1897, had very little education himself because of helping his parents farm in Montgomery County.

Noah Noble home, Brookville.

Claude Matthews, Indiana governor (1893–97), married the daughter of James Whitcomb, who had been governor fifty years earlier.

The first Indiana governor to die in office was Ashbel P. Willard, who suffered a lung hemorrhage in 1860 while making a speech in Columbus.

Willis Van Devanter of Marion was one of three Hoosiers to serve on the U.S. Supreme Court, appointed (although as a Wyoming resident) in 1911 and remaining for twenty-six years; the second was Sherman Minton of New Albany, appointed in 1956 and serving seven years. Both retired from those posts. The third was John G. Roberts Jr., who grew up in Long Beach, Indiana, and was appointed in 2005.

Governor George N. Craig, whose controversial administration included criticism for refusal to pay a state bonus to Korean War veterans and a state highway scandal involving his former aides, helped form the National Mental Health Association.

Seeking a U.S. Senate seat in 1944 because the Indiana Constitution prevented him from a second term as governor, Henry F. Schricker rejected an offer from Franklin D. Roosevelt to run for vice president. Roosevelt switched to Harry Truman, who became president when FDR died in April 1945. Schricker did not win the election to the Senate either.

Shortly before former governor M. Clifford Townsend died in November 1954, he won two shooting matches with a muzzle-loading rifle at Friendship in Ripley County.

Warren T. McCray, convicted in 1924 of mail fraud while governor of Indiana, spent his prison time editing the convict publication *Good Words* and teaching a Sunday school class. He was pardoned in 1930.

David Gerard, nationally known cartoonist who drew *Will-Yum* and later *Citizen Smith*, served on the city council of his hometown of Crawfordsville and was mayor from 1972 to 1975.

Davis Floyd, for whom Floyd County is believed named, was a familiar figure in public affairs in southern Indiana. Due to his association with conspirator Aaron

Burr, Floyd was fined and sent to jail, but a few days after his sentencing he was elected clerk of the lower house of Indiana's territorial legislature.

When William Hendricks ran for governor of Indiana (serving 1822–25) he was unopposed, the sole gubernatorial candidate to have no opponent in the state's history.

Brookville, noted as the home of several government officials, had few families to equal the Nobles for political service. Ben was a doctor and state representative; Lazarus directed the federal land office; James served in the Indiana General Assembly and the U.S. Senate; and Noah was Indiana governor from 1831 to 1837.

Stephen Harding of Ripley County served for a short time as governor of the Utah Territory during the Civil War.

Indiana once had laws: prohibiting throwing confetti at a person or object; providing a fine for theater owners who let in patrons wearing a hat, cap, or bonnet; barring keeping a horse, cow, calf, swine, sheep, or goat in an apartment; fining persons dropping banana peels on the street; prohibiting quarrels with one's wife on Sundays; banning hammocks without babies in them in any park; and levying fines for people living in Indianapolis who had more than one cow.

In 1935 legislators from Lake County introduced a bill in the Indiana General Assembly to make Lake County a separate state, highlighting the Calumet Region's feeling of being at odds with the rest of Indiana. The bill made it to second reading before its impracticality was recognized.

Thomas N. Stilwell of Anderson, who served in state and national legislative bodies and as U.S. minister to Venezuela 1867–68, was president of First National Bank of Anderson and was killed in a gun battle. Stilwell was dueling with a person he thought was responsible for his indictment for embezzlement.

Three artists each did the portraits of six Indiana governors after Governor Conrad Baker commissioned the portraits in 1869. Two artists who each did six portraits were Hoosiers, but the third was a Canadian. When the portraiture began, pictures were used by the artists for the thirteen former governors who were dead.

No mayor served in that office in Indiana longer than Eugene "Beaner" Linn of Gas City in Grant County. Linn first won the office in 1967 after suing for a recount against the Democratic incumbent in the primary election. He was reelected in every subsequent election until his death on February 11, 2001, at the age of sixty-six.

Marie Theresa Lauck of Indianapolis was the first woman to serve in the Indiana General Assembly in both the senate, 1964–68 and 1972–76, and the house, 1959–60.

A law went into effect on July 1, 1929, that taxed chain stores in Indiana. It was signed by Governor Harry Leslie and was amended in 1933. It required an annual licensing fee on a sliding scale of $10 for a person operating five to ten stores and up to $25 for someone operating more than twenty stores. The amendment raised to $150 the license for each store in excess of twenty.

Grave Consequences

The grave of William Tuffs in Elkhart County marked the site of the only participant in the Boston Tea Party to be buried in Indiana. Tuffs migrated to the Hoosier State in 1839 and died in 1848 at the age of 108 at the home of a daughter and nephew fifteen miles northeast of Goshen.

A Native American cemetery near Lebanon contains the bodies of Miami Chief Chapodosia and Chief Dixon, who fought to the death over a Thorntown treaty. The chiefs are buried in ceremonial dress, seated, facing each other.

Edmund Hadley, whose home in Coatesville is a landmark, died of a heart attack on Memorial Day 1878, at the age of fifty-three. Two later owners of the house, Mrs. William Dean and Virgil Osborn, also died of heart attacks on Memorial Day.

The mausoleum of Caleb Smith in Crown Hill Cemetery in Indianapolis is empty. Smith, a lawyer, newspaper editor, state legislator, congressman, and secretary of interior under Abraham Lincoln, was buried in Greenlawn Cemetery in Indianapolis before Crown Hill was created. His widow erected a mausoleum, but fearing grave tampering, she did not move Smith's body into the Crown Hill edifice. In fact, his burial site in Connersville, where the body was taken in the late 1860s, is unknown.

Connersville dentist John Doughty saved the teeth he pulled in the late 1800s and cemented them into the form of a pyramid to serve as his grave marker, encased in glass. This was done at his death, but later the teeth were stolen and only the glass case survived to be mentioned in Fayette County histories. Nobody knows who extracted the grave marker.

Linda J. Jones of Linwood created a pet cemetery in her yard because she took in thirty-three cats during a blizzard in 1978 and kept them until they, and nineteen more cats she took in, died one by one.

At Hope in Bartholomew County the Moravian cemetery has all the grave markers laying flat to demonstrate the Moravian belief that everybody is equal in death. Also, the cemetery has sections for men, women, and children instead of interring all members of a family in graves near one another. Similarly, at New Harmony the Rappites demonstrated their belief of equality in death with a cemetery that has no headstones at all and, for the same reason, there are no records on the locations of any graves.

It is said that John G. Heinl haunts Highland Lawn Cemetery in Terre Haute and so does his bulldog. The loyal pet refused to leave the mausoleum where Heinl was buried in 1920, and when the dog died the family interred it in the mausoleum, too.

Harold J. Holmes was buried not only in the wrong grave in 1986, but also in a grave already occupied. About three months after his interment, his family found out that an unknown Native American, probably a pauper, already had been buried in the grave in Oaklandon Cemetery. The body of Holmes later was moved to the plot he actually had purchased before his death, about three graves away from the Native American.

In 1965 Ernest E. Bauermeister of Fort Wayne invented a vertical casket, an aluminum cylinder that he said could save space because five could be used in the space occupied by one regular horizontal casket.

Sylvester W. Sammons, owner and publisher of the *Morristown Sun*, was the first person to commit suicide from the Soldiers and Sailors Monument in Indianapolis when he jumped from the west side on February 2, 1932, in despondency over his health. He had owned the newspaper only one day. The first death on the monument occurred in 1912 when Bobby Polsgrove, three years old, strayed from his mother and toppled through one of the windows.

When John Allcorn was crushed to death by a poplar tree he was chopping down, a seven-foot portion of the trunk was sawed off and hollowed out for a coffin. On the burial site in Grouch Cemetery near Gnaw Bone, a poplar shoot appeared at the head of the burial mound and grew into a living tree monument.

The last will of Alfred Charles Kinsey, the Indiana University researcher on human sexuality, was a review of his goals and obstacles. It read: "From the beginning of our own research there have been many persons who have gone out of their way to try and prevent our securing histories from particular groups . . . the most important thing for us to establish right now is the right of the scientists to engage in such research."

When Pearl Bryan of Greencastle was murdered and decapitated, her body was buried at Greencastle, but her head was never found. Cincinnati dental students Scott Jackson and Alonzo Walling were convicted of the murder in Kentucky, where the body had been found, but they never told what happened to the head. Jackson said he had epilepsy and couldn't remember. Walling said Jackson had hypnotized him, so he drew a blank too. The Bryan case got national attention and inspired a ballad.

When Virgil C. Kidd was crushed to death while working under a 1966 Chevrolet Corvette in 1972 in his Crawfordsville business, Kidd's Quality Used Cars, his grave marker was a model of a Cadillac Sedan DeVille, the kind of car he had owned most of his life. It is the only known such gravestone in the United States, with its accurate proportions of the car.

Musician Michael Jackson of Gary in 1987 tried, unsuccessfully, to buy the skeleton of John Merrick, known as the elephant man and subject of a movie in 1980, to add to Jackson's collection of the unusual at his California home. Merrick died in 1890 in London, and his skeleton was kept by a London hospital.

Ida Ditmire of Fulton became the first licensed embalmer in Indiana after being the only woman in the otherwise all-male class that took the state examination in 1905. She and her husband Frank built a new funeral home in Fulton in 1908. She let children in the family skate in the room above the funeral home where coffins were stored.

When a gravestone was purchased to mark the grave of Jonathan Jennings, Indiana's first governor, the body was moved from its unmarked site into Charlestown City Cemetery. But in 1981 the marker was moved farther back in the cemetery lest it be harmed or stolen from its position over the grave near the cemetery entrance. A less conspicuous marker was placed over the actual grave site.

Green Hill Cemetery in Bedford is unmatched anywhere in its examples of the stonecutter's art applied to rare grave markers, which include a life-size stonecutter's bench, complete with tools, and other statues and carvings.

A mummy, which had been in the Wayne County Historical Museum at Richmond since 1929, was x-rayed at Reid Hospital in Richmond in 1974, showing that the mummy was a female, missing a lower jaw, having only five teeth, and probably too tall for her sarcophagus because her chest was broken to compress her size. The mummy had been purchased by collector and museum founder Julia Meek Gaar of Richmond on her seventh trip to Egypt. It already had been on display in Cairo for about forty years when Gaar acquired it.

Industry

Frank B. Shields, who came to Indianapolis in 1913 from Seymour, invented a brushless shaving cream, which he named Barbasol.

The first Hoosier to get a letter through Rural Free Delivery was E. A. Jones, who got the delivery near Hope from Raleigh Norman on October 15, 1896.

One bicycle made in Indianapolis in the late 1800s was called the Ben Hur.

The nation's first exposition on street paving, with contractors and manufacturers showing their wares, was held in Tomlinson Hall in Indianapolis April 1–5, 1890, sponsored by the newly formed Commercial Club. The club developed into the Indianapolis Chamber of Commerce.

Alvah C. Roebuck, born in Lafayette in 1864, answered a newspaper employment ad while working as a watchmaker in a jewelry store in Hammond. The ad had been placed by Richard W. Sears in Chicago, and a famous mail-order catalog partnership was created when Roebuck got the job.

The steam carpet cleaning industry in Indianapolis, and probably Indiana, was born when Howard's Steam Carpet Cleaning Works opened on February 4, 1876.

When Van Camp Seafood Company in Indianapolis ran the first full-page food ads in some national magazines in 1894, the ad offered free sample cans of Van Camp Pork and Beans for six cents each.

Although the Rappites of New Harmony drank only wine and cider, they made five hundred gallons of beer a day and could make thirty-six gallons of whisky daily—all of it exported to points as far away as New Orleans.

At a site once called Armour Town at Cedar Lake, Peter Scholl operated a shoemaker's shop, where his grandson, William Scholl, served an apprenticeship at age seventeen. Doctor William Scholl later was famous for his foot comfort aides, still sold under the Scholl name.

C. E. Woolman of Bloomington was the main founder of Huff Daland Dusters, a crop-dusting company that later became Delta Air Lines.

In 1984 U.S. Steel Corporation in Gary poured its 350 millionth ton of steel, which, company officials said, made it the most productive steel plant in the world.

The Smith Brothers operated a cough drop company in Michigan City from 1919 until 1945, one of their two sites in the United States.

Washington C. DePauw, whose name is immortalized in DePauw University, made his fortune in ventures, which by 1881 earned him the description "the nerviest businessman in Indiana."

Once upon a time, when messages were passed to moving trains by means of a forked stick, the High-Speed Delivery Fork Company at Shelbyville was a one-man factory manufacturing the forks.

Omar bread, made in Indianapolis for many years, took its name from the Omar Khayyam poem that contains the lines, "a loaf of bread, a jug of wine and thou."

Before its depletion, natural gas in Indiana gave rise to seventy-one glass factories, all operating by 1905 during the natural gas boom, making the state the second largest producer of glass in the United States. Dunkirk had eleven glass factories during the natural gas boom; Greentown, about thirty miles away, had only one glass factory, but its products are more famous today than any produced by Dunkirk's eleven plants.

At one time a total of nine furniture factories operated in Shelbyville, including the Davis-Birely Company, which was once the world's largest maker of tables.

An effort to grow mushrooms commercially inside Marengo Cave in the mid-1980s failed because cave crickets kept eating the crop.

A decade of reports started in 1869 by Edward Travers Cox, one of the early state geologists and director of the geological survey, was one of the first collections of information designed to attract industry to Indiana to develop natural resources.

Colonel Harland Sanders, who became the famed Kentucky Fried Chicken king, was born in Henryville and lived much of his youth in Clark County.

Mineral wood, or rock wool, was manufactured in Indiana beginning in 1897 and once was the product of as many as sixteen industrial plants in the state.

Coal, mined in Indiana starting in the 1830s, was used mainly for steamboat fuel until about 1850. The first coal shaft in Indiana was dug by John Andrews, a coal operator from Scotland, in Clay County in 1845.

By 1908, or fifty-six years after its incorporation, the Haskell-Barker car company in Michigan City was building fifteen thousand railroad cars a year. It merged with the Pullman company in 1922.

Colonel Harland Sanders.

Maurice Thompson, besides being a soldier, civil engineer, naturalist, lawyer, legislator, poet, editor, literary critic, and novelist (he wrote *Alice of Old Vincennes* in 1901), also was Indiana's state geologist from 1885 to 1888.

The vineyards at Vevay, begun in 1802 by Swiss settlers, were the first successful commercial vineyards in the nation.

Elmer Cline, vice president of Taggart Baking Company, "wondered" at the sight of balloons traditionally released at the Indianapolis Motor Speedway. He adapted both the balloons for a packaging design and the awe about them for the name of a new Wonder Bread developed at the Indianapolis bakery in 1920. The bakery was bought by Continental Baking Company in 1925.

The bricks used to pave the Indianapolis Motor Speedway in 1909 came from Veedersburg, once a major producer of bricks.

Courtesy of Fred Cavinder

Eli Lilly Company, Indianapolis.

Colonel Eli Lilly started his pharmaceutical company in Indianapolis with $1,400 cash and three employees.

Studebaker at South Bend, once a wagon maker, produced eleven thousand wagons a year, causing it to claim the title of the world's largest wagon works.

Kingsford Heights near La Porte was created during World War II to house workers for the adjacent Kingsburg Ordnance Plant, which had twenty thousand employees during production for World War II.

Indianapolis Chain and Stamping Company, forerunner of Diamond Chain Company, was producing 60 percent of the bicycle chains in America at the turn of the twentieth century.

The United Auto Workers became an international union at a convention in South Bend in April 1936.

A streetcar drawn by mules and horses, which was started in 1892 between Brownstown and the nearby community of Ewing, was the last such conveyance in the state when it halted operation in 1916.

The first female factory inspector in Indiana was Mrs. Arthur T. Cox of East Chicago, appointed a deputy state factory inspector on January 30, 1918, by Governor James P. Goodrich as the state geared up for loss of men in World War I. Cox, working under inspector John J. Walsh, earned $1,500 a year. There were then about fifty thousand women employed in Hoosier factories.

Inventiveness

Andrew J. Moyer, born in Pulaski County in 1899, is one of two Hoosiers in the National Inventors Hall of Fame at Akron, Ohio. (The other is aviation pioneer Wilbur Wright.) Moyer, a microbiologist, developed a method for industrial production of penicillin, which played a part in the drug's vital increased production during World War II. Moyer died in 1959 at age fifty-nine with ten U.S. patents and twenty scientific publications to his credit.

Kokomo claims to be the first place in the nation for fifteen events or products—everything from wartime ordnance to tableware and, of course, Elwood Haynes's automobile.

"Dollar Day," an advertising sales gimmick popular in the mid-1900s, was developed by Carl Suedhoff of Fort Wayne.

Burtis L. Dickman, once the mayor of Auburn, invented a submarine in 1958 designed to photograph sunken vessels for insurance claims.

Lodner D. Phillips invented a hand-propelled submarine in 1852 that could be operated by one passenger using one hand to turn a propeller and the other hand to operate a tiller. Phillips developed four subs tested on the Great Lakes near

Michigan City from 1845 to the 1850s, but none was completely successful, and Phillips could not interest the navy in his underwater crafts.

Thomas Edison is said to have worked in the Western Union office in Union Station in Indianapolis in 1864 on the graveyard shift, having been fired at Fort Wayne as a Western Union apprentice.

A standardized Texaco service station, prevalent in the 1930s, was designed by Walter Dorwin Teague, a native of Decatur. About ten thousand of the stations were built, with four variations, before Texaco began a redesign in the 1960s, shortly before Teague's death.

The Coca-Cola bottle, created at the Root Glass Company in Terre Haute in 1915, was one of the first two containers patented by the government because of its distinctive shape; the other was the Haig and Haig pinch bottle.

A self-propelled tricycle, considered the first gas-powered conveyance in the United States, was manufactured in Anderson starting in the mid-1890s at Lambert's Buckeye Manufacturing Company, originally established in Ohio. The Lambert in question, who died in 1952 at the age of ninety-two, held an estimated six hundred patents.

In 1858 Benjamin Murkley Nyce, a professor at a college founded at Hartsville in 1850, invented the Nyce Fruit House, a forerunner of refrigeration.

Charles L. Henry, whose mule line in Anderson developed into a network of electric railways, became known as the father of the Indiana interurban; some say Henry coined the word "interurban."

Doctor James Slyter of Fulton County invented fiberglass.

In 1938 the federal government organized Deshee Farm Inc., a farm cooperative in Knox County, as an experiment in new economic and social ideas following the Great Depression. The farm had forty-two dwellings, nine barns, three machine sheds, and ten poultry houses. Beset by problems and locally called "Little Russia" by some, the farm lasted seven years with such constantly changing tenants that only two farmers remained there the full time. Federal bickering and changing times were ultimately blamed for ending the experiment.

Alexander Samuelson came up with the idea for the shape of the Coca-Cola bottle.

A filling station owner in Hope advertised by marking telephone poles with yellow paint, creating a trail to his business. The venture is memorialized in the Hope Yellow Trail Museum.

While serving as manager of the Nashville House in Brown County, Portia Howe Sperry designed a rag doll that was named Abigail after a Brown County pioneer woman and became a nationwide best seller. The doll, created during the Great Depression, was marketed by, among others, Marshall Field and Company in Chicago and L. S. Ayres and Company in Indianapolis. Sperry also wrote a book based on the Abigail doll.

Warren North of Brookston was the inventor of the first automatic feeding system for cattle in 1959 and also was the first person in Indiana to host the Farm Progress Show twice—in 1958 and 1964 at his Green Ridge Farm.

Leslie Haines, a Carmel native, developed an electric traffic signal, one of the first in the nation, which was installed at Range Line Road and Main Street in Carmel in 1923 and remained there ten years.

The railroad bridge over the Wabash River in Carroll County was replaced in 1949 by a revolutionary method; seven spans of the old bridge were removed one at a time and dismantled in the river as a new span was set in place. The system caused almost no interruption in rail service.

In the fall of 1985 a bridge was built beside an old bridge on Indiana 7 at Vernon, and for the first time in Indiana the new bridge was rolled into place on Teflon rollers, moving a total of 39 feet. The span was 528 feet long.

Gertrude Muller of Fort Wayne developed a folding toilet seat usable by babies or adults and began manufacturing them in an old barn in Fort Wayne. The firm, Juvenile Wood Products Inc., later became the Toidey Company. Once it got an order from Bob Hope for his two adopted children, causing Muller to say, "There's plenty of glamour in my business."

In the late 1800s Richmond claimed to be the lawn mower capital of the world.

Micajah C. Henley of Richmond made major contributions to roller skating by inventing the ball-bearing skate wheel and a toe clamp operated by a key instead of a screwdriver. Henley skates were in use from 1884 until World War II.

A washing machine called the Favorite was patented in 1882 and made in Middletown by James Gronendykes. It was sold nationwide, including by Sears Roebuck and Montgomery Ward.

Christian Vossler of Mitchell created several inventions in the 1880s and 1890s, but his invention of an airtight wooden barrel lined with shoemaker's wax to bottle sunshine was a complete failure. The only thing it did successfully was to get Vossler mentioned in some histories of the area.

Industrialist Ermal Cleon Fraze, a native of Delaware County, invented a way to attach pull tabs to the tops of beer and soft drink cans after being frustrated in 1959 on a picnic without any can openers. He sold the rights to the Aluminum Company of America. His invention was replaced in the 1970s by a nonremovable tab, still in use today.

Ralph Teetor of Hagerstown invented an automobile cruise control, lock mechanism, fishing rod holders, and an early lawn mower, although he was blinded in an accident when he was five years old. He was president of Perfect Circle Company.

In 1893 Harold Urey of Walkerton, a graduate of Kendallville High School and Earlham College, discovered the heavy isotope of hydrogen, which made possible the hydrogen bomb and brought him a Nobel Prize and honors and doctorates from twenty-five universities in five countries on three continents.

The first all-metal clarinet, made by Charles Gerard Conn of Elkhart, had the patent number 410,072, obtained August 27, 1889. Before that clarinets had been made of wood.

Letters

John Finley, whose 1833 poem "The Hoosier's Nest" in the *Indianapolis Journal* was a major factor in solidifying the nickname "Hoosier" for Indiana citizens, was not a Hoosier. His father was a merchant in Virginia when sixteen-year-old John headed west and ended up in Richmond after being in several other locations.

Ben-Hur, famed novel by Lew Wallace, sold only 2,800 copies in the first seven months after it was published, but six years later, in 1886, sales were 4,500 a month, and by 1911 sales had surpassed one million. In 1913 Sears Roebuck ordered one million copies at thirty-nine cents each for catalog sales.

James Whitcomb Riley, who became not only a poet, but also a successful vaude-ville performer and lecturer, was unable to speak before classmates in high school because of intense stage fright.

Although many insisted that James Whitcomb Riley wrote the mildly risqué poem, "The Passing of the Backhouse," the verse actually was written by Charles T. Rankin, who was a Riley contemporary and admitted trying to copy the Riley style. The poem was copyrighted in 1946, and copies were sold at the Indiana State Fair in 1956. Rankin's great-granddaughter, Kathleen Rankin, renewed the copyright on the poem, which at one time had been illustrated by her father, also named Charles T. Rankin.

Novelist Booth Tarkington as a child was a close friend of James Whitcomb Riley, nearly twenty years his senior, after the pair became acquainted at Tarkington's Indianapolis home. Riley was a suitor of Tarkington's older sister, Mary Booth "Haute" Tarkington. Booth Tarkington and Riley corresponded for years.

Only one Hoosier, Booth Tarkington, has won two Pulitzer Prizes for fiction. Other double winners have been William Faulkner and John Updike.

Booth Tarkington, who by 1912 had become an alcoholic, changed to a teetotaler when told by his doctor and his new wife, Susanah, that drink was interfering with his writing. One result was *The Flirt*, a novel published in 1913.

As a young man Indianapolis author-to-be Booth Tarkington was best man at the wedding of fellow Indianapolis author Meredith Nicholson to Eugenia Kountze of Omaha, Nebraska.

Novelist Booth Tarkington served in the Indiana House of Representatives in 1902, having beaten his Democratic foe in Marion County by about 3,500 votes. His campaign had been considered a joke by many, but his election was guaranteed in such a Republican stronghold. He served one term.

One of the world's most popular poems in the last quarter of the nineteenth century, "The Curfew Shall Not Ring Tonight," was written by Rose Hartwick Thorpe, a native of Mishawaka, who did not copyright it and lost a large income from the ballad, popular in America and England and translated into seventeen languages. Thorpe, born in 1850, wrote the verse after being inspired by a magazine story. The ballad tells how a young girl saves her lover from execution by using her body to halt the curfew bell, which would have signaled his execution.

Author Gene Stratton-Porter's first article was published without her getting paid because the publisher had lost her address. After she communicated with him again, she was sent the money—sixteen dollars.

Gene Stratton-Porter was named Geneva, but started calling herself Gene when she and her husband, Charles Porter, moved to Geneva, Indiana, evidently not desiring confusion between her real first name and the name of the town. Although forever linked to natural areas and wildlife, she died on December 6, 1924, in an auto crash near her home in Los Angeles, far from wilderness.

Limberlost State Historic Site (Gene Stratton-Porter home), Geneva.

When Gene Stratton-Porter began writing, she rented a post office box in her own name since mail was delivered to her husband Charles Porter's drugstore at Geneva. That way nobody would know if she had failed by seeing her manuscripts being returned. Similarly, she avoided sending stories to magazines that appeared on the shelf at the drugstore.

It is said Wendell Willkie would never have written his book *One World* after his defeat for president in 1940 without the urging of *New York Herald Tribune* book section editor Irita Van Doren, who was Willkie's mistress.

John M. Hay of Salem coauthored with John G. Nicolay a ten-volume *Abraham Lincoln: A History*. They got $50,000 from *Century* magazine for a serialization of the material, a considerable sum of money in 1890. Hay, secretary of state under President William McKinley and President Theodore Roosevelt, also wrote poems that appeared in *The Oxford Book of American Light Verse*. They were titled "The Pledge at Spunky Point" and "Good and Bad Luck."

Hoosier author Jessamyn West, who went to California at the age of six, attended a Sunday school in Yorba Linda taught by President Richard M. Nixon's father, somewhat ironic because Nixon's mother, Hannah Milhouse Nixon, was born in Indiana near Vernon. West was born at North Vernon.

David Graham Phillips of Madison, a well-known reporter and writer, was fatally shot on a New York City street in January 1911 by musician Fitzhugh C. Goldsborough, who then killed himself. Police found that Goldsborough had written threats to Phillips and had grown insane over the belief Phillips had used the Goldsborough family as the basis for his books. Phillips, however, never had met the Goldsboroughs, and his books were totally fictional.

May Wright Sewall was a nationally known suffragette and promoter of women's rights, who came to Indiana in the 1870s. She reported about her spiritualist experiences with, among others, her deceased husband Theodore in a 1920 book titled *Neither Dead nor Sleeping*.

Charles A. Beard, born in 1874 near Spiceland, owned and edited his own newspaper in his hometown of Knightstown when he was only eighteen years old. Beard became a noted teacher and historian at Columbia University and published more than sixty books on historical, social, and political subjects.

Augusta Stevenson, who wrote twenty-nine volumes in the popular Childhood of Famous Americans series, was born at Patriot in 1870 and started her literary career as a playwright in 1908. She did not retire from writing until she was 104.

When Knighthood Was in Flower, published in 1898 and written by Charles Major of Shelbyville, is said to be the first best seller promoted by a national advertising campaign.

A brick house on Indianapolis's Monument Circle was the birthplace in 1840 of Fanny Van de Grift, who later married Robert Louis Stevenson and traveled with him to the South Seas. She also was given credit by Stevenson with inspiring some of his literary works. Van de Grift died in 1914, and her ashes were taken to Samoa.

Winifred Sackville Stoner, born in 1902 at Evansville, at three years of age knew music, at four learned Latin, at five wrote stories and jingles for newspapers and magazines, at six started a writing campaign to save forests near Evansville, at twelve passed college entrance exams, and eventually wrote twenty books. But she never attended school, being tutored at home by her mother.

The novel *Roxy*, written by Edward Eggleston and published in 1878, has characters modeled after citizens of Vevay, Indiana, the author's birthplace.

Edward Eggleston's *The Hoosier School-Master*, the first great novel by a Hoosier, was published in serial form in *Hearth and Home*, a magazine that he was editing at the time. The novel was issued as a book during the same year in New York. Eggleston also wrote several histories of the United States and considered his greatest honor his election in 1900 as president of the American Historical Association.

George Cary Eggleston, younger brother of Edward Eggleston, was a popular literary figure in his own right, but was overshadowed by Edward, author of *The Hoosier School-Master*, and was largely forgotten after his death.

Famed author Ring Lardner had his first writing job in Indiana, working as a reporter and sports editor for the *South Bend Times* at twelve dollars a week in 1906.

James Walter Hervey, besides being considered the father of the Indiana State Board of Health, also was the first Indiana writer to create horror stories, writing *The Scroll and Locket; or, The Maniac of the Mound* in 1858.

Sarah T. Bolton, an Indiana poet whose home was in Beech Grove in Marion County, lived for two years in Geneva, Switzerland, where her husband Nathaniel was sent as U.S consul by President Franklin Pierce.

Indiana's first poet is said to have been a Mrs. Lard, who in 1823 published "The Banks of the Ohio" while in Vermont, but nobody seems to know for sure who Mrs. Lard was.

Reuben Kidder, a lawyer at Paoli and Corydon, produced the first confessional writing in Indiana called *The Life and Adventures of John Dahmen: The Murderer of Frederick Nolte and John Jenzer*. It consisted chiefly of oral confessions and declarations taken down while Dahmen was in prison. Published in Jeffersonville in 1821, the work also contained a brief statement on the murderer's trial and execution.

Captain James Riley, a surveyor in Adams County, wrote a book in 1817 about his enslavement in Africa by Barbary pirates, which is said to have influenced Abraham Lincoln's feelings about slavery.

Author Meredith Nicholson reportedly called the Brown-Kercheval House in Rockport the "House of a Thousand Biscuits," a parody of the title of his book (*House of a Thousand Candles*), because of the hotel owner's generosity to him when he stayed there.

The oldest book in the Hugh Thomas Miller Rare Books Room at Butler University is a 1473 volume printed in Italy, a treatise on legal reasons for excommunication.

The Saint Joseph County public library became the first library in the United States to operate a World Wide Web server on the Internet, commencing March 14, 1994.

Zerna Sharp, born near Frankfort, developed the format for the famous Dick and Jane books used to teach millions of children to read, but she never married and had no children of her own. She was a consultant for Scott Foresman Publishers in Chicago.

John Cain's *Miscellaneous Poems* was the first complete book of poetry published in Indiana and written by a Hoosier, but no copy of the volume, printed in 1832 in Indianapolis, is known to exist.

Paul Dresser was forty when he wrote "On the Banks of the Wabash, Far Away"; Mary Jane Ward was forty when she wrote *The Snake Pit*; Lloyd Douglas was fifty-two when his first novel, *The Magnificent Obsession*, was published and sixty-six before *The Robe* was published; Lew Wallace didn't publish *Ben-Hur* until he was fifty-two.

Joseph L. Hensley, longtime attorney and judge in Jefferson County, used cases in the court and his private practice as the basis of more than twenty mystery and suspense novels.

Theodore Dreiser of Terre Haute was almost as noted as a philanderer as he was an author, seducing Yvette Szekely Eastman of Hungary in 1930 when she was sixteen and he was fifty-nine, and continuing to correspond with her until his death in 1945.

When George Ade became wealthy as an author he often sent his royalty checks to his father, cashier at the Kentland bank, so the checks could be shown to Kentland residents, who had said sending George to college had been worthless.

Indiana's first published cookbook was *Mrs. Collins' Table Receipts; Adapted to Western Housewifery*, printed in 1851 using material written by Angelina Maria (Lorraine) Collins of New Albany.

John Guedel, a native of Portland, was a writer for the Hal Roach Studio in Hollywood, became a major radio writer-producer, and in 1938 originated singing commercials for radio.

A statue at Shelbyville represents not a real person, but a fictional character, Balsar Brent, from the novel *Bears of Blue River*. Brent is sculpted with his pet bear cubs Tom and Jerry.

The most complete collection in the nation of early writings on South Pacific native culture is housed at the Butler University Rare Books Room. They were collected by William F. Charters, who lived his adult life in Indianapolis and gave his collection to Butler, with which he had no known association.

James Buchanan Elmore, known as the bard of Alamo (Indiana) for his doggerel poetry, once ran for the Indiana legislature conducting his campaign in rhyme.

He lost, for which there obviously was a rhyme and reason. He also once gave testimony in court in rhyme, answering a charge he had tapped sugar trees on Sunday.

Although little remembered, Henry James O'Brien Bedford-Jones wrote more than one hundred mystery and romance novels to become one of Indiana's most prolific authors. None of the books was a critical success.

Hoosier Janet Flanner, who wrote from Paris under the pen name Genet for *The New Yorker* magazine, received the French Legion d'Honneur April 5, 1948. She had been cited for the award in 1947 but failed to attend the presentation ceremony.

Some have speculated that when Harriet Beecher Stowe visited her brother, Henry Ward Beecher, in Indianapolis for several weeks in 1844 she found the prototype for Uncle Tom in her famed novel *Uncle Tom's Cabin*. Her brother took her several times to meet a black man, Uncle Tom Magruder, who lived at the corner of Noble and Market streets in Indianapolis. Stowe never acknowledged him as the model for her book, although she took notes on the conversation and surroundings.

Holly G. Miller, a professor at Anderson College, and Dennis E. Hensley, a free-lance writer at Fort Wayne and a professor of writing at Taylor University, wrote seven books by long distance in the 1980s and 1990s. Four books were mystery-romances, and three were books on writing. Miller and Hensley sent chapters back and forth to each other by mail for collaboration in the early days; more recently they found that e-mail made the twin writing chores simpler.

Miscellaneous

In 1854 cattle were driven through Attica as part of a longhorn cattle drive from Texas to New York, an operation headed by Tom Candy Ponting and Washington Malone.

Archaeologist Heinrich Schliemann, who discovered and excavated the sites of ancient Troy and Mycenae, lived in Indianapolis for a few months in 1869 to use Indiana law to obtain a divorce from his Russian wife and select a mail-order

Greek bride. In Indianapolis Schliemann owned a house at College and Washington streets, among other property.

The "Jones Twins," as they were known, born in Tipton County on June 24, 1889, had a head at each end of one trunk, four legs jammed together, and arms in the normal place. They were exhibited publicly and died in February 1891.

Robert Holt of Indianapolis escaped from a sunken submarine in the 1930s when the sub, being tested, took water and dropped 150 feet to a reef off Delaware. Since it was 231 feet long, the tail stuck out of the water and Holt and the rest of the crew escaped through a hole cut in the tail.

Alice J. Dunler of Delphi, the first woman telegraph operator in the world, was one of the personal pupils of Samuel F. B. Morse. She later served thirty-three years as manager of the Western Union office in Peru before her retirement about 1910.

Starting in 1919 a two-year hunt was conducted by U. G. Leedy, president of Leedy Drum Company, to find two hides large enough to build the seven-foot Purdue University drum.

At the age of ten, Thomas Day was given an 1858 half dollar carved with the initials W and G. Day gave it to his son, Sam Waller Day, in 1924. The son kept it until it fell from a special bag in his pocket and was accidentally spent in 1949. Later, in a grocery store he ran in Evansville, he handed change to bread delivery man Ace Weber, who noticed the coin had the initials W and G carved on it. The coin had come back to Sam Day after a twelve-year absence.

Jimmy Risk of Monticello, boy wonder of horseshoe pitchers in the 1920s, won seven state titles, made a livelihood by pitching horseshoes at shows, and once demonstrated for President Harry S Truman at the White House. He toured with Gene Autry on the rodeo circuit and, among other tricks, lit a match with one toss and put it out with a second toss.

The *Polish Cavalcade of Music* on station WJOB-AM in Hammond started in 1929 and still was broadcasting on Sundays in 1991, its sixty-fifth year. The show was started by Eddie Oskierko, who was joined in 1952 by Walter Skibinski. Skibinski became sole host in 1984.

According to legend, Martin Piniah, who lost all his property in 1945, lived for years under the Little Calumet River viaduct in East Chicago and was known as "the troll under the bridge." He got a bath, new clothes, and dinner at least each Christmas Eve courtesy of the Salvation Army.

A needle one and one-half inches long used in quilting was removed from a knot that appeared on the arm of I. A. Defenbaugh of Greenfield in February 1934, thirty-four years after he had swallowed it when he laughed while holding it in his mouth.

In the 1937 flood, which affected much of the southern half of Indiana, a parrot of Mr. and Mrs. George Jetta of Louisville showed up at Mitchell. Its vocabulary included "Get me out of here," "Don't let the water touch me," and "Why didn't you bring a boat?"

At New Albany during the 1937 flood, three men, C. K. Gregg, C. T. Allen, and Eddie Metzker, became godfathers to a baby born on a pool table under lights provided by a generator.

In the 1937 flood, which hit twelve states and brought death to 137, Raymond Katz of Chicago, a watercolor artist commissioned by the Red Cross to paint flood scenes at Evansville, used flood water to do his paintings.

Helen Artie Belles, known as Nellie, was born in Spencer in 1856 and was the mother of Harold Macmillan, who became British prime minister. Belles was married to Maurice Macmillan of the publishing firm Macmillan and Sons. She was his second wife and met him while in Paris studying voice. Harold Macmillan visited Spencer in 1956.

Commander Malcolm D. Ross of Linden, a 1941 graduate of Purdue University, ascended 113,740 feet from the deck of the USS *Antietam* on May 4, 1961, one of eight flights he made via balloon into the stratosphere. He spent ten years in the office of Naval Research. With him on the May ascension was Lieutenant Commander Victor E. Prather.

In 1944 a self-service automatic laundry was started in South Bend, the first of the new Laundromats in Indiana. It was a decade before they became popular.

Charlene McGuire and Rita Jane McGuire, both of Muncie, were the first Hoosiers as mother and daughter and maybe the first in the nation to take the oath together to practice law before the U.S. Supreme Court on May 7, 1951.

Irene Faust, her husband William H. Faust, and her son William H. Faust Jr., all of Indianapolis, became the first mother, husband, and son to ever be admitted to practice law before the Supreme Court in 1940.

A two-headed baby born at Petersburg on December 12, 1953, lived several weeks. Only one of the heads seemed normal. The twin bodies shared a single spine but the heads moved, slept, and ate independently of each other.

For more than twenty-five years, up into the 1970s, the Rock Island Refining Corporation on the north side of Indianapolis used a herd of goats to control grass and weeds among the storage tanks.

According to reports, Hoosier spy William King Harvey of Danville showed President John F. Kennedy a secret agreement between Fidel Castro and Nikita Khrushchev on nuclear threats, a revelation that was a prelude to the Cuban missile crisis in 1962. Harvey, a member of the CIA, had stolen the document from Castro's safe. For his trouble he was reassigned to Rome.

The first eagle born via artificial insemination in captivity in Indiana was hatched in April 1974 at the home of Don Anderson in Brazil. Born under nonlaboratory conditions in an incubator, the eaglet came from eggs laid by an eagle called Cry, fertilized by a male called Grindle.

The first person chosen Indiana Senior Queen via a statewide contest was Alice M. Bird of Fort Wayne, sixty-nine years old when crowned in August 1974. Before that senior queens had been informally picked from visitors to the Senior Citizens' Building on the state fairgrounds on the basis of age.

Altha Cravey became the first woman in Indiana admitted as a journeyman electrician in the International Brotherhood of Electrical Workers after completing the required eight thousand hours of job training in a program at the Indiana Vocational Technical Institute at Bloomington in 1980. Her first job was helping install the Christmas lights on Monument Circle in Indianapolis.

About 1983, Hoosiers who joined International Dull Folks Unlimited included Thomas F. Watts of Indianapolis; David Adam and Kris Pangborn of Jeffersonville; Vivian R. Barber, resident of the Indiana Masonic Home at Franklin; Richard D. Cannon of Evansville; and Howard M. Watts of Garrett.

In 1989 former Indiana governor Edgar Whitcomb (1969–73) left Tel Aviv, Israel, to sail around the world in a series of cruises in a thirty-foot single-mast sailboat. He completed the trip in August 1996 at the age of seventy-eight. On some legs of the journey he sailed fifty-five days without seeing another boat.

At the time, no one older than Crocky Wright had ridden a motorcycle through flaming pine boards, as he did July 14, 1990, at Lincoln Park Speedway at Putnamville at the age of seventy-one. "I'm glad it's over with. I don't want to do it anymore," said Wright, who had been a racer and motorcycle daredevil since the 1940s.

Jim Barber of Indianapolis, training in the White River, won New York's 28.5 mile Manhattan Island Marathon Swim on August 10, 1991, against forty-two competitors.

In mid-August 1992 David S. Bowman and Angela K. Thurman, both of Huntington, were married and bungee jumped from a 120-foot tower. They had won a contest sponsored by Holiday World Amusement Park at Santa Claus, Indiana, and an Evansville radio station. The Bowmans had lived together for four years and had two children, one born three weeks before they bungee leaped into matrimony.

In November 1992 seventeen-year-old Spencer Hamner of rural Edinburgh, became the eighth boy in the family to become an Eagle Scout, the highest rank in scouting and a national record. Hamner was a member of a Shelbyville troop.

Laura Marie Carmody was born in Humana Hospital in Indianapolis on January 9, 1993. Her father, Dan Carmody, also was born on January 9 and so were her grandfather, John Carmody Jr., and her uncle, John Carmody III.

The birth dates of Donald Duane Carter, born February 24, 1959, in Saint Francis Hospital in Indianapolis; his father, Donald C. Carter; his grandfather,

George M. Carter; and his great-grandfather, Richard R. Carter, all were the same.

Cole Porter had dinner parties at 11 p.m. regularly in the posh Waldorf Astoria in New York, where he lived, and he often had one of his favorite foods—spaghetti.

The LE & W (Lake Erie & Western) Railroad, part of the Nickel Plate system in Indiana, was nicknamed the Leave Early and Walk, a slam at the railroad's passenger service.

John W. Collings of Lizton gained reentry into the United States after a trip to Peru, for which he had forgotten his passport, because he had relatives who were killed in the Pigeon Roost massacre in Scott County in 1812. An immigration official who happened to be from Scottsburg verified that Collings was a U.S. citizen because Collings knew of the massacre and the Collingses who were killed there; therefore the official let Collings back into the United States.

Nature

When the earth's continents shifted thousands of years ago, a coral reef was left that extended from Louisville to Indianapolis. The large area of the reef that was exposed at the Falls of the Ohio River was the world's largest exposed fossil reef of its kind.

When the glacier began to recede twelve thousand years ago, it formed Lake Chicago, which covered areas that now are Indiana beaches. Lake Chicago, the predecessor of Lake Michigan, was some sixty feet higher than Lake Michigan is now, but its waters escaped west, eventually flowing into the Mississippi River.

One of the most noted cave explorers in the mid- to late 1800s, Horace Carter Hovey, was a native of Rob Roy and was a clergyman before he took up cave exploration.

Around the turn of the twentieth century, New Castle became known as the Rose City because of giant American Beauty roses that gave rise to some eighty-five greenhouses in the town. Failure of natural gas supplies used to heat the greenhouses and a destructive tornado ended the New Castle rose era.

E. Gurney Hill and his son Joseph developed an estimated 75 to 80 percent of all indoor roses grown at one time in the United States through their Richmond firm, Hill Floral Products Inc.

In the great 1811 earthquake that affected what is now Indiana, researchers report that 1,874 aftershocks were felt from December 16 into March.

Meteorites have been found in Indiana in Harrison County, 1859; Kokomo, 1862; Franklin County, 1866; Rochester, 1876; Vermillion County, 1883; Plymouth, 1893; La Porte, 1900; South Bend, 1915; Lafayette, 1931; Rush County, 1948; Starke County, 1959; and Seymour, 1976.

There is said to be a memorial in Brown County showing where the last deer was shot in 1897 by Repp H. Pane, who was hunting squirrels and shot a deer when it appeared. The location of the memorial is kept secret, however. Although deer are plentiful in modern times, especially in Brown County State Park, they were scarce, believe it or not, in the late 1800s and hadn't been seen for years. Legend says that Pane carved a picture of the deer on a rock and put the mark of a bullet above it.

William Temple Hornaday, a native of Plainfield, became chief taxidermist at the Smithsonian Institution in 1882 and a founder of the National Zoo in Washington in 1889. He also was the first to document the presence of crocodiles in Florida.

Indiana has more energy underground in the form of coal than the entire United States has in gas and oil, experts at Purdue University have reported.

Unlike other lakes in Indiana, Bass Lake in Starke County is elevated, occupying the top of a ridge; it is fed by springs and wells.

Charles Deam of Bluffton, known as the first state forester in Indiana and the first to catalog all trees native to the state, was a college dropout. A total of seventy-one plants were discovered by Deam or named in his honor.

Charles Deam, when he learned a rare oak tree was scheduled to be razed, bought the third of an acre on which the tree stood and in 1915 deeded it to the state, making it a preserve set aside for a single tree. The oak, Quercus X. Deamii Trelease, was discovered October 9, 1904, northeast of Bluffton along Indiana 116 by Lent A. Williamson and became popularly known as the Deam Oak.

Charles Deam, who recorded such things, reported that there are, or at least were at one time, 124 species of trees native to Indiana, including seventeen species of oaks. Deam's foxglove, named to honor the noted botanist, has been reported in other states, but the reports have proven false, making the plant indigenous only to Indiana.

A dune called the Hoosier Slide at Michigan City was nearly two hundred feet high and visible from Chicago until it was leveled between 1890 and 1920 for use in glassmaking and landfill.

A huge twelve-foot-high stump, rescued from a hundred-foot-high tree that was struck by lightning on the T. A. Harrell farm near Kokomo, was hollowed out to be used as a phone booth and could hold twenty-four people.

John Muir, whose name is linked with great areas of nature conservation such as Muir Woods in California and who lost sight in his right eye in an industrial accident in Indianapolis, started out as a very successful inventor. He credited his successful recuperation in Indianapolis with becoming interested in nature.

The famed tree on the tower of the courthouse at Greensburg is the twelfth aspen to grow there. The first tree, appearing 1865–70, probably came from a seed planted by a bird.

The morning of April 3, 1972, was the time of the sighting of the last prairie chicken in Indiana. The prairie chicken, about the size of a pheasant, was first seen in the late 1600s by explorers in the Midwest.

Those helping Jacob Whetzel cut a trace through the wilderness in Marion, Johnson, Morgan, and Shelby counties, camped one night by a stream in Shelby County. Whetzel, joining them, produced a bottle of peach brandy that he had acquired in Owen County for just such a time—the supplies running out and

Decatur County Courthouse, Greensburg.

THE INDIANA BOOK OF TRIVIA

Fred Cavinder

the determination flagging. The drinking of the brandy caused them to then and there name the stream the Brandywine, one of the prettiest in Shelby County.

Governor Harold W. Handley signed a law in 1957 changing the Indiana state flower from the zinnia, chosen in 1923, to the peony. Before that the state flower had also been the blossom of the tulip tree or tulip poplar and the carnation. The choice of the peony was supported by, among others, a peony grower who was in the Indiana House of Representatives. No other state has named more flowers at one time or another as the state floral emblem.

In one of the best land deals in Indiana, territorial governor William H. Harrison paid Indian tribes $10,000 and a small annuity for three million acres in southern Indiana.

Indiana was visited by glaciers three times, experts say, well before the time that Hoosier hospitality was warm enough to melt them.

For years it was said that movement of sand on Mount Baldy, a shifting dune near Michigan City, made a sound like a bass fiddle when the wind was right.

At least twelve Indiana caves from Bloomington to the Ohio River provided salt-peter needed for gunpowder for American forces to fight the British in the War of 1812.

At Lake Galatia near Fowlerton in Grant County, discovery of a nearly complete mammoth skeleton in 1904 prompted a lawsuit. It resulted in the ruling that the skeleton belonged to the farm owner as real estate rather than to the tenants as personal property. The skeleton was sold to the American Museum of Natural History in New York.

Crosley State Fish and Wildlife Area is named for the land's owner, Powell Crosley Jr., a Cincinnati industrialist and sportsman, who once owned the Cincinnati Reds baseball team and radio station WLW. He sold 4,084 acres to the state in 1958.

When the huge Constitution Elm in Corydon was sawed up, a victim of disease in 1925, it created thirty-four wagonloads of wood that were eventually made into souvenirs.

USS Constitution *Grove.*

Two groves of white oak trees at the Crane Naval Weapons Support Center (Crane Division, Naval Surface Warfare Center) were dedicated in 1976 for use in refurbishing the USS *Constitution*, known as Old Ironsides. It gets repairs every twenty-five to thirty-five years and requires about 340,000 board feet of oak just for replanking.

Frank Etherton of Madison had a pet bass in a pond at his rural home in the late 1980s that took earthworms from Etherton's hand. The fish became so well known Etherton was invited to take it on the *Tonight Show Starring Johnny Carson*. Etherton declined. After a few years the fish vanished—the victim of age, disease, or poachers.

A sycamore near Worthington, once proclaimed the biggest deciduous tree in the nation, stood 150 feet high with a trunk 43 feet around until it was destroyed by wind and lightning. Part of a branch survives as a memorial in Worthington's city park.

The leaf of the devil's walking stick reaches sizes of five feet long and three feet wide, making it the largest leaf of any Indiana plant.

So many black squirrels have lived around Goshen and elsewhere in Elkhart County that they are honored by the Black Squirrel Golf Club on the west side of Goshen. The black squirrel, the product of a recessive gene in the eastern gray squirrel, was brought to Goshen by Ernest Martin in the 1930s from Michigan. He set them free after keeping them in captivity for four years. Today the black squirrel still exists in the area and some nearby regions, and it has crossbred with the gray squirrel, producing some mixed offspring.

In eight months of a reduced diet and exercises of running laps and doing push-ups and deep knee bends, Bunny, an elephant at the Mesker Zoo in Evansville, lost 640 pounds, dropping to only 7,200 pounds.

In February 1963, Spiceland was invaded by so many skunks that the Associated Press and United Press sent the story across the nation, and reporters from all over Indiana converged on the town to cover the oddity.

Although a Pennsylvanian, Doctor Alton A. Lindsey, while professor of plant ecology at Purdue University from 1947 to 1973, earned the title "father of Indiana nature preserves." He helped found the Indiana Chapter of The Nature Conservancy. In 1933 Lindsey traveled to the South Pole with the Admiral Richard E. Byrd expedition; he was honored by twelve islands in Antarctica being named the Lindsey Islands. Purdue formed Lindsey Field Laboratory at Ross Biology Preserve.

Twin Swamps in Posey County near Mount Vernon is one of the few areas in Indiana where the spider lily is in bloom each August and is the only Hoosier site for the world-endangered globe mustard plant.

People

It was rumored that Thomas Posey, territorial governor of Indiana from 1813 to 1816, was the illegitimate son of George Washington, but the evidence is circumstantial. It was strong enough, however, to be noted in an early history of Posey

County, which was named in Posey's honor. The Posey and the Washington families were neighbors at one time.

In one of the longest civil trials in Indiana, five nieces and nephews sued over the estate of Maude Huntington Darrach, widow of the wealthy founder of the Interstate Car Company, Eugene Darrach. The case resulted in a hung jury in Indianapolis in 1943 and was retried in Danville in 1945, where it took three weeks to choose a jury and five months to hear the case. It was decided in favor of the defendants—Indianapolis Public Library, two churches, thirteen nephews, and other relatives and friends of Maude. At stake had been an estate of about $1.5 million. The panel in the trial became known as the "long jury."

William Shirley Williams, born in southern Indiana, became a western scout and helped lay out the Santa Fe Trail in 1825–26.

Sir Henry Worth Thornton, knighted by King George V for his aid to British railroad shipping in World War I, was born in Logansport in 1871 and attended grade school there.

The Indian chief LaFontaine, who lived near Huntington, weighed 368 pounds and used a specially made chair three and a half feet wide between the arms.

As president of the State Bank of Indiana, Judge Samuel E. Perkins regularly counted the silver coins held by the bank in the mid-1800s by lifting each barrel, which held $500 worth. Once he noted a shortage of twenty-five cents, according to legend.

Ikot Alfred Ekanem was installed as prince of the Ibibio nation in southeast Nigeria at Indiana University during a ceremony televised worldwide in 1966. He lived and worked in Indianapolis for nearly twenty years after that. His nation contained about a million subjects, whom he ruled by correspondence and occasionally commuting from Indianapolis to Nigeria.

Sherman Minton of New Albany had an unusual career that included serving in the legislative branch of government as a U.S. senator, 1934–40; as part of the executive branch as administrative assistant to President Franklin D. Roosevelt; and as part of the judicial branch as a member of the Seventh Circuit Court of

Appeals, named in 1941, and as a Supreme Court justice appointed by President Harry S Truman in 1949.

John and Richard McGriff of Adams County died within less than a year of each other, Richard in 1899 and John in 1900. At the time they were the oldest twins in Indiana, both ninety-six years old.

Ambrose Bierce, writer and satirist who grew up near Warsaw, was the youngest of twelve children whose names all began with the letter *a*.

When he died in 1960, Sol Strauss, a Jewish immigrant from Germany, left the fortune of $1.3 million he made in his dry goods store on the town square in Paoli to that community to be used for civic improvements.

Karolyn Kilmer Holloway of Frankfort was the first woman on the Indiana State Fair Board, serving from 1945 to 1954.

At one time Noble County had both the largest and smallest men in Indiana. George W. Walker, born in 1850, was five feet, ten inches tall and weighed 501 pounds, and Jesse Allen, born in 1880, reached adulthood at thirty-seven inches tall, weighing 80 pounds.

Allan D. Thom, who is buried in Fredonia in Crawford County, was famous in that area because he wore a raincoat all year and also never drank water. That's what legend says.

The Jewish population in Ligonier grew to two hundred by 1880, making it unusually large in such a small Indiana town, and dropped to zero in 1981 with the death of Durbin Mier, the town's last Jewish resident.

Levi Coffin, whose Fountain City house was part of the Underground Railroad, moved to Cincinnati in 1847 and then to England in 1864, where he organized the Freedmen's Aid Society. In 1867 he was a delegate to the International Anti-Slavery Conference in Paris.

George Ash, who built the oldest surviving brick house in Indiana (1798–1803) on the Ohio River near Vevay, was captured at age ten during an Indian raid

George Ash house, near Vevay.

on his family's homestead in North Carolina and lived seventeen years with the Shawnee Indians.

The first "Hoosier" honored on a postage stamp was Father Jacques Marquette, who traveled along Lake Michigan in what is now the Calumet Region in 1674. Marquette, whose name is honored with a park in the Indiana Dunes, was featured on stamps in 1898 and 1968. The next Hoosier honored on a stamp was General George Rogers Clark in 1929. Clark led an army that seized Fort Sackville for the United States at Vincennes in 1779.

Journalist Ernie Pyle divorced his wife Jerry in 1941, hoping it would jar her out of her brooding, drinking, and using sedatives. It didn't. The Pyles remarried a year later.

Nellie M. McNeal of Monroeville in Allen County had more than one hundred pen pals all over the world, and sometimes on her birthday (she was 101 years old in January 1990) she would get more than two hundred cards and letters.

THE INDIANA BOOK OF TRIVIA

Her appearance on the *Tonight Show Starring Johnny Carson* in 1989 brought her thirty new pen pals.

Hoosier television sportscaster Chris Schenkel had a totem pole carved from a dead white oak tree at his Indiana home on Lake Tippecanoe. But when the carver inexplicably carved two large female breasts on one totem figure, Schenkel had a double mastectomy performed on the totem to calm his upset wife Fran, a former June Taylor dancer.

Television sportscaster Chris Schenkel was one of an eleven-member high school graduating class at Bippus in Huntington County.

Edith Briggs, a lifelong resident of Fulton, was at one time the sole Hoosier member of the Eight Years without a Birthday Club. She was born on February 29, 1896, at Grass Creek and had no birthday anniversary until February 29, 1904, the next leap year. She died in 1975.

On September 27, 1984, Chris Hearne jumped rope 1,845 revolutions in ten minutes, a record and a rate of more than three revolutions per second. The stunt was in the lobby of the American United Life Building in downtown Indianapolis. A device in the rope handle counted the revolutions.

Orville Redenbacher, the Indiana popcorn king, played sousaphone in the Purdue University marching band from 1924 to 1926.

Clifford Relander of Danville was adopted by the Wanapum band of the Yakima Indians and was the first white man buried by the Yakima on their reservation in the northwest when he died in October 1969. Relander spent more than forty years as an adviser, counselor, and champion of the rights of the Yakima nation.

New York newspaper editor Horace Greeley disliked Indiana because in 1853, missing his train in Lafayette en route to a speaking engagement in La Porte, he rode to Brookston on a railroad freight and livestock car and traversed the eerie Kankakee swamp at night on a handcar he commandeered.

Frank B. Shields, who developed Barbasol shaving cream, donated land in 1937 for a new gymnasium at Seymour, his hometown. Shields later lived near Martinsville. His will of 1944 bequeathed Foxcliff, his palatial estate near Martinsville, to the state of Indiana for a governor's mansion, with adjoining lands as a state game preserve.

When Ada Elizabeth Worland was born in Indianapolis in 1900 weighing only a pound and a half, she was not expected to live, since babies requiring incubation outside a hospital rarely survived in that era. Her makeshift incubator, consisting of a wooden crate placed near an oven and fitted with Mason jars filled with hot water and a flat tin filled with hot water as a "mattress," made news around the world. Married to Norman Lang, she lived well past her seventy-seventh birthday.

Stephen J. Hannagan of Lafayette became a world-renowned press agent who made the Indianapolis Motor Speedway famous, popularized Sun Valley and Miami Beach, and became a celebrity on Broadway and in Hollywood.

G. Gordon Liddy, famed figure in the Watergate scandal, once worked as an FBI agent in Indianapolis.

Before Blanche Stuart Scott became the first woman to fly solo in an exhibition at Fort Wayne in 1910, she made a cross-country motor trip to promote Overland autos; after the Indiana flight and additional airplane exhibitions, she became a writer and radio commentator in Hollywood. She told the press that her first public flight at Fort Wayne could have been longer, but her instructor, Glenn Hammond Curtiss, had forbidden her to make turns until she had mastered straight flight.

Frances Wright, who fought for liberal causes at New Harmony with Robert D. Owen, died after slipping on a patch of ice in her front yard.

Alfred Kinsey, whose sexuality research at Indiana University startled the world in 1948, did not date women until he was twenty-seven years old and married the first girl he dated steadily.

Richard M. Helms, internationally prominent as director of the Central Intelligence Agency from 1965 to 1973, once worked as a reporter for the *Indianapolis Times*.

A postage stamp honoring Elvis Presley made its national debut on January 8, 1993, at Market Square Arena in Indianapolis, the site of Presley's final concert on June 26, 1977. Presley died in August of that year.

William Conner, whose homestead near Fishers is now Conner Prairie Pioneer Settlement, married Mekinges, the daughter of Delaware chief Anderson. But Mekinges went west with her people in 1820, and Conner then married Elizabeth Chapman.

Diane Keaton, who grew up in Morristown but only to the height of 5 feet, 1½ inches, was cofounder in 1988 of the National Association of Short Adults. It had some fifty members and a newsletter called *The Short Sheet.*

In 1990 Parke County, known as the covered bridge capital of the world, elected a sheriff named Mark Bridge.

Wendy's founder R. David Thomas, an orphan adopted by Rex and Olivia Thomas of New Haven, Indiana, began his career as a busboy at the Hobby House Inn in Fort Wayne about 1948. Thomas met Colonel Harland Sanders in Fort Wayne and urged him to sell his chicken in buckets. Later Thomas took over failing Kentucky Colonel franchises in Columbus, Ohio, sold the chicken franchises in 1964, and used the proceeds to start his first Wendy's.

Thomas Lloyd Posey, once Indiana adjutant general and an Indiana General Assembly representative from Harrison County, never married, but raised fourteen orphans in his Corydon home.

John Morton-Finney of Indianapolis at age 106 was the oldest practicing attorney in Indiana and probably in the nation. He also had eleven college degrees, five of them in law. In 1991 he was inducted into the National Bar Association Hall of Fame in Washington, D.C. He died in 1998 at the age of 109.

The embalming of Man o' War, said to have been a first for a racehorse, was part of a funeral conceived by former New Albany newspaper editor James Galloway. Working for a wire service in Lexington, Kentucky, when Man o' War died in 1947, Galloway suggested the embalming, which used twenty-three bottles of preservative.

Booth Tarkington started to talk at seven months of age, not by saying mama, but by calling the family dog.

General William Kepner of Miami in Howard County, an army air corps officer who took part in record-setting balloon ascensions, did not get his high school diploma until he was fifty-three years old.

Clark Campbell, a butcher at Nashville, lost his entire accounts receivable unexpectedly one day when his nephew, Paul Percifield, painted the butcher shop walls. Campbell kept customer records on the wall, crossing out and remarking figures of credit and payments as they occurred. Percifield thought he was doing a good deed by painting over the messy figures.

D. C. Stephenson, leader of the Ku Klux Klan in Indianapolis and Indiana in the 1920s, insisted on being called "the old man," although he was only in his early thirties.

Harriet Colfax, cousin of U. S. vice president Schuyler Colfax, was keeper of the lighthouse at Michigan City for forty-three years, retiring in 1904 at the age of eighty.

Early Lake County settlers, fearing they would lose their land when it was officially sold by the government, formed a squatters union in 1836 and successfully intimidated bidders at an 1839 land auction by brandishing knives and rifles.

When Jennie and George Conrad settled in Newton County in the 1880s, Jennie took such a dislike to Lake Village that she used Morocco as her address and sent a horseman the thirty-six-mile round-trip to Morocco rather than let the Lake Village postman deliver her mail.

One of the first white men to visit what is now Indiana, explorer René-Robert Cavelier de LaSalle, had a lieutenant, Henry de Tonti, who wore a metal prosthesis to replace his right hand that had been blown off in an explosion.

Bill Holman of Crawfordsville wanted to be a fireman, but when he grew up became a cartoonist and created a comic strip about Smokey Stover, a fireman.

When Miami war chief Francis Godfroy died in 1840, then the second richest Native American in Indiana, he was owed $15,000 by New York merchants who had purchased furs from him.

Lighthouse, Michigan City.

Metea, chief of the Potawatomi near Fort Wayne, was poisoned to death in 1827, allegedly at the hand of fellow Indians who objected to his adherence to the 1826 treaty with the whites.

The image of Hugh McCullough of Fort Wayne appeared on the twenty dollar bill in 1902, a tribute to his post as the nation's first comptroller of the currency, a post he took in 1863 to inaugurate the new national banking system.

Silas Schimmerhorn, a fugitive from Morgan's Raiders in the Civil War, is said to have taken refuge in Bat Cave in what is now Versailles State Park, coexisting with timber wolves, living off the land and never being seen, captured, or discovered even in death.

George Boyden, a traveling salesman, took his own life on December 28, 1900, by jumping into a kitchen cistern in Newburgh and drowning. He did this, according to reports, because Mary Ann Castle, known as "marrying Polly," had refused to wed him a third time. Boyden had been the fourth and sixth husband of Polly, who married at least eight times, some say seventeen times.

Doctor George Washington Buckner Sr., born a slave in Kentucky, attended school in Indianapolis, the Indiana State Normal School at Terre Haute, and Eclectic Medical College in Indianapolis. He set up practice in Evansville and in 1913 was appointed by President Woodrow Wilson to serve as minister to Liberia (1913–15).

Chief Jean Baptiste Richardville, a Miami Indian leader, was so large that when he died in 1847 his body had to be taken through a window of his home near Huntington to lay in state.

Jacob Gumbel, sales manager for the Brock Hat Factory in New Lebanon near Carlisle, delivered a special silk hat to John W. Davis of Carlisle, who became Speaker of the U.S. House of Representatives in 1844. President-elect James Polk saw the hat, asked that one be made for him, and wore the topper from New Lebanon on inauguration day, March 4, 1845.

Johnny Horine, who shinned shoes at Hagerstown, started visiting national and international expositions in 1876 and continued his travels until the Chicago Exposition of 1933. He earned the name of the globe-trotting bootblack.

Edward A. Hannegan of Covington was named minister to Prussia in 1849 and dazzled the queen. But when he kissed her hand in public, Frederick Wilhelm IV jealously seized on a point of etiquette and demanded Hannegan's recall. Hannegan was sent back to Covington in 1851.

Lew Wallace of Brookville, later of Crawfordsville, was a member of the court that tried the conspirators in the assassination of Abraham Lincoln. Henry Smith Lane, also of Crawfordsville, was a delegate active at the Republican National Convention that had nominated Lincoln for the presidency.

Betty Beeman and her daughter Anita Freehauf of Lakeville started a registry in 1988 for Vietnamese potbellied pigs based on the same guidelines as the American Kennel Club for dogs.

The first Mrs. America from Indiana was Rosemary Murphy of Kentland, who won the crown on June 10, 1960. However, by the 1980s the pageant headquarters in California had wiped out all records prior to 1977 so there is no official record of her crowning. She later moved to Florida and went into the real estate business.

Jane Todd Crawford, the first woman to have an ovariotomy, underwent the surgery in 1808 without an anesthetic. She later moved to Graysville in Sullivan County to live with her son, dying there in 1842.

Issachar Bates was one of the zealots who founded a Shaker community near Oaktown in 1808, adhering to the Shaker beliefs in pacifism, communal property, and celibacy. But before adopting celibacy, Bates fathered eleven children.

Doctor Chaim Weizmann, who developed synthetic acetone for the British in World War II, used royalties from production of the product in Commercial Solvents Corporation at Terre Haute toward fulfilling his dream of founding a state of Israel. He became Israel's first president.

Jane Dale Owen, daughter of Robert Owen of New Harmony fame, had three sons with her husband Robert H. Fauntleroy. The sons not only married in a triple wedding in 1837, but also took their honeymoon trips together.

Clessie L. Cummins, who founded Cummins Engine Company in Columbus in 1919, was a chauffeur in the household of William Irwin, who financially supported the Cummins firm. Cummins was considered a wizard at mechanics.

John Matthews of England, whose creation of the first limestone industry near Ellettsville in 1862 caused the town's population to swell, built a French mansard-style home, still standing, which has the faces of his four children carved over the front door.

Ban Johnson, known as the creator of the American baseball league in 1900, is buried in Spencer because he came there in 1927 to retire in the hometown of his wife.

Herb Shriner, the comedian who came to Indiana "as soon as he heard about it" and made the state a major part of his homespun humor, named his daughter Indy Shriner.

Ernest Moore "Dick" Viquesney not only created *The Spirit of the American Doughboy*, a statue that stands in his hometown of Spencer, he also was said to have designed more war-related statuary than any other American sculptor.

Ban Johnson gravestone, Spencer.

THE INDIANA BOOK OF TRIVIA

William Montgomery Crane, for whom the 62,000-acre Crane Naval Weapons Support Center is named, was the first chief of the Bureau of the Navy, named in 1842. He killed himself four years later. He was distraught because he had refused to attend the testing of a new "Peacemaker" gun, which exploded during test firing aboard the *Princeton*, killing the U.S. secretary of state, the secretary of the navy, and several others.

The Spirit of the American Doughboy, *Spencer.*

John B. Stetson, the hatmaker, married Elizabeth Shindler of Orleans and gave her parents a house, precut in Philadelphia and erected in the Orange County town of Orleans in 1894. Still standing, it is one of the first prefabricated houses in the Midwest.

Ormsby McKnight Mitchell, railroad engineer and surveyor for whom Mitchell is named, entered West Point at the age of fifteen and taught there by the time he was twenty.

John L. Lewis, president at one time of the United Mine Workers, had his office in the Merchants Bank Building in Indianapolis in the 1920s.

C. Carey Cloud, Nashville-based painter, was known as the Cracker Jack artist because he devised many of the playthings found in Cracker Jack boxes. He also designed toys given away on radio programs such as *Little Orphan Annie* and *Superman*.

Prefabricated house, Orleans.

John Lusk, who at the turn of the twentieth century owned land that became part of Turkey Run State Park, slept in a barrel as protection against "hants."

For a brief time, Orpha Nusbaum of Goshen was the world's oldest living person. In January 1988 she gained the status at 112 years old after the death of a 114-year-old in Pennsylvania. But on March 30, 1988, Nusbaum died in a nursing home at the age of 112 years and 7 months.

In 1940 two men at Angola, garage owner Charles M. Griffin and attorney Kenneth Hubbard, organized the Screwballs of America and incorporated it the next year when groups elsewhere wanted to form chapters. What happened to the organization is something any screwball can tell you.

In 1944 songwriter Hoagy Carmichael's mother, Lida, was made an honorary grandmother by the Grandmothers War Bond League.

The ashes of Otto Paul Klopsch and his wife Mathilda Swicker Klopsch were scattered by their son at a sundial on the Indiana University campus in Bloomington after their deaths in 1935 and 1937 because they met at the sundial in 1896 as students and fell in love at first sight. The university placed a plaque commemorating the romantic site and the spreading of their ashes at the sundial, located between Maxwell Hall and the Student Building in the old part of campus.

Julie Nixon Eisenhower came to Indianapolis every week in the 1970s in her job as an editor at the *Saturday Evening Post*, which also published *Jack and Jill, Child Life, Children's Playmate*, and *Young World*. The daughter of President Richard Nixon and his wife Pat, she was accompanied by Secret Service men who tried to remain unobtrusive as Eisenhower pursued her special interest in stories for children. She did most of her work for the magazine from her home at the time in Bethesda, Maryland.

The United States Jaycee Women voted to disband while meeting in Indianapolis on June 17, 1985. The vote of 212–26 eliminated the organization as of July 1 that year.

Max M. Shapiro created the nation's first cafeteria-style delicatessen when he established Shapiro's Restaurant on South Meridian Street in Indianapolis in

Julie Nixon Eisenhower.

1940, which became a landmark in the city. Shapiro, known as "the deli man," was memorialized with the Max M. Shapiro Restaurant Excellence Scholarship after his death.

Places

Swayzee (Grant County) notes two proud claims. Its basketball team set a state tournament record of nine overtimes in beating Liberty Center, 65–61, in the regionals at Marion in 1964, and Swayzee is said to be the only town in the world named Swayzee.

Oil found at the turn of the century at shallow depths in Jasper County inspired the founding of a town called Asphaltum. Both the town and the oil boom were short lived.

At Jonesboro (Grant County) the Tracy Tavern was used between 1872 and 1895 for checker tournaments for skilled players from Indiana, Ohio, and Illinois. The tavern later was a secondhand furniture store, then was made into apartments.

The Indiana Highway Commission once changed the name of Gnaw Bone (Brown County) to West Point, but the new name was never accepted.

Both the Calumet area of Indiana (Lake County) and the Calumet River are named for an Indian ceremonial pipe, often termed a peace pipe, which in French was called a calumet.

Indiana has approximately twenty-three million acres of land.

A street on the south side of Franklin in Johnson County is named Champs Ulysses because veterans of World War I wanted to honor the famous avenue in Paris, which is named Champs Elysees. It sounds similar to the Franklin street name but refers to the Elysian Fields in Greek mythology.

Beverly Shores, a town on Lake Michigan in Porter County incorporated in 1947, had only one resident twenty years earlier.

In February 1988 the Fort Wayne board of park commissioners declined to rename Orff Park, .02 of an acre, in honor of Carole Lombard, the 1930s Hollywood star and wife of Clark Gable. She had lived near the park before leaving the city. Lombard died in a 1942 plane crash while returning to Hollywood after selling war bonds in Indianapolis.

For two decades after its erection in 1928, Butler Fieldhouse in Indianapolis (famed as the longtime site of the Indiana state high school basketball tournament) was the largest gymnasium in the nation.

In the 1920s when Cedar Lake was a resort area luring Chicago gangsters, tourists, and the socially prominent, it was fringed by forty-two hotels. None of them survived successfully into the twenty-first century.

Chesterton was incorporated in 1869 but, because taxes were insufficient to support a town, unincorporated in 1878. It didn't reincorporate until 1899.

Madison has both the oldest fire department in Indiana and the oldest firehouse still in use, but they are not one and the same. The oldest department, Fair Play Fire Company No. 1, was organized in 1841, but is no longer in its original headquarters. That leaves Washington Fire Company No. 2 as the occupant of the state's oldest firehouse, which was erected in 1848, two years after the company was organized.

Waldron (Shelby County) was so named because a resident going to a meeting to discuss changing the name from Stroupville found a scythe blade in a field that was made by the Waldron Scythe Company in Ohio.

Gosport is the only town in Indiana on the famed Ten O'clock Treaty Line. It was a shadow line cast by an Indiana spear stuck in the ground at 10 a.m. in 1809 used to mark land to the south, retained by the Indians, and land to the north, sold to the government by the Indians.

In Beech Grove there is an intersection of Rodney and Dangerfield, but nobody seems to know why the names of the comedian were used for Rodney Court and Dangerfield Drive.

Fair Play Fire Company No. 1, Madison.

Mellott, after a community campaign, began flying the U.S. flag at 80 percent of the Fountain County town's homes, prompting the Indiana General Assembly in 1971 to designate Mellott as "Flagtown, USA."

Big Foot, Ratsburg, Old Sixteen, Chiseltown, Spray, Transylvania, Rhodes, Hindostan, Dicksburg, Spicklepoint, and Dot were all once Indiana towns that faded into ghost towns and then disappeared.

Rockville writer Juliet V. Strauss is credited with helping save the area that is now Turkey Run State Park by alerting state officials that the area was about to be bought and the trees cut down by a lumber company. She had a column in the 1920s in the *Ladies' Home Journal.*

Clay County, which had numerous manufacturers of clay products such as bricks in the last half of the 1800s, was not named for its clay soil, but for the famed statesman Henry Clay.

The label "Crossroads of America" was pinned on Indianapolis in 1925 by the National Geographic Society.

Ligonier in Noble County is said to have been founded by Isaac Cavin, although he never lived there; the town was named after a town in Pennsylvania.

Ten Indiana counties bear the names of men who fought in the Battle of Tippecanoe in 1811, including John Tipton, who in 1829 acquired the ground at the battle site to erect a monument to memorialize the conflict.

Kokomo was named to honor the Indian chief Kokomo, and a monument is erected there in his honor. But it isn't at his grave. The location of his grave site has remained unknown since the cemetery was moved to make way for Kokomo High School and some neighboring houses.

The town of Ladoga was named by young people who found a Russian lake called Ladoga described in a geography book.

Fountain Square in southeast Indianapolis once was called The End because it was the terminus of the mule-pulled cars on the streetcar line.

Chief Kokomo monument, Kokomo.

The Scottish Rite Cathedral in Indianapolis was designed using thirty-three feet or multiples of thirty-three for its dimensions to be symbolic of the number of years Christ was on earth.

Haughville, a section of west side Indianapolis, gets its name from Benjamin F. Haugh, who moved an iron-casting factory there in 1875.

When Greensburg registered thirty-five degrees below zero—an Indiana record—on Groundhog Day 1951, the city fathers moved the weather station to the municipal waterworks, hoping warmer readings there would forestall the possibilities of the town acquiring a frigid reputation.

It is believed that Moscow in Rush County was named for the city in Russia, but nobody knows why.

The crown of Crown Hill Cemetery in Indianapolis is not the highest point in Marion County, as many believe. The zenith is at a point near the far northwest corner of the county.

Crown Hill Cemetery is one of the few cemeteries listed on the National Register of Historic Places, an honor bestowed on it in 1973.

Visitors to William Conner, whose home is now part of the Conner Prairie Pioneer Settlement, included writers Washington Irving and James Fenimore Cooper and fur baron John Jacob Astor.

The Hamilton County Courthouse is noted for, among other things, being the site of the sensational 1925 trial of D. C. Stephenson, the Ku Klux Klan leader, for the murder of Madge Oberholtzer.

Noblesville may have been named to honor U.S. senator James Noble or Lavinia Noble, the fiancée of Josiah F. Polk, one of the platters of the town.

Roberts Settlement was created in Hamilton County by Hansel Roberts in 1838 as a haven for people who were a mixture of black, white, and Cherokee blood. During the 1890s the residents left, many going east. Roberts is buried in a cemetery that survives there.

Pumpkinvine Pike, where Elwood Haynes tested his first automobile outside Kokomo, is now Boulevard Street.

As the winner of a shooting match, Colonel John B. Duret is said to have gained the honor of naming the new Cass County seat and chose Logansport, for Logan's Port at the confluence of the Wabash and Eel rivers.

Temple Israel in Lafayette is believed to be the oldest surviving synagogue in Indiana; it was built in 1867.

When the Indianapolis Children's Museum prepared its opening exhibit on December 7, 1925, one problem to be dealt with was a donated live alligator. The museum was the third museum for children opened in the United States.

When Tell City ordered a statue of William Tell and his son Walther in 1974, city fathers never expected it would become a target for thieves. Artist Donald B. Ingle of Evansville was transporting the statue he created in a rented van when he had to pause overnight because of mechanical problems. When he awoke he found the van and statue missing. Both were recovered in Cleveland a week later without a clue as to who took them or why.

When the G. H. Hammond Company, a Hammond packinghouse, burned on October 23, 1901, covered in the $500,000 in damages were 4,500 freshly slaughtered pigs. The firm did not rebuild.

In 1920, when East Chicago and Indiana Harbor had a population of mostly single men or married men without their families, the area had 110 saloons.

Merrillville in Lake County was established at the spot where sixteen Indian trails once converged. One was the Sauk Trail, a main artery between Fort Dearborn (Chicago) and Detroit.

Up to 116 passenger trains passed daily through Indianapolis's Union Station before railroad travel waned in the United States.

Wanatah, a village in La Porte County, was allegedly named for an Indian chief noted for his laziness. His name, Wanatah, is said to mean "keep knee deep in mud."

In 1985 Fort Wayne was selected as an All-American city and also was voted the most livable city by the U.S. Council of Mayors. No other city got both honors in a single year.

The name of Glen Miller Park in Richmond does not refer to the famed orchestra leader of pre-World War II days, but instead to the glen that once was owned by Colonel John F. Miller and later became part of the park.

In recent times Fairmount had one former resident listed in *Who's Who in America* for every 230 residents in the town, a ratio fourteen times the national average. Three of the notables were college presidents.

Fairmount claims, with little proof, that the Eskimo Pie was developed there, and that Orlie Scott built an auto there, wrecked it, and sold it to Elwood Haynes, who repaired it and added a brake, the absence of which perhaps might explain Scott's wreck.

Matthews in Blackford County was so busy during the glassmaking boom at the turn of the nineteenth century that it had ten glass factories, other plants, five hotels, two banks, and more than one hundred business and professional offices, and it induced the Indianapolis professional baseball team of the Western Association to relocate there in 1901. By 1908 everything, including prosperity, had left town.

Orland in Steuben County, thought to be the oldest town in the county, was named by opening a hymn book at random.

An Allen County village called Hamilton, founded in 1849, was renamed Leo in honor of Pope Leo XII, for whom a church in town also was named.

Huddleston House as an inn on U.S. 40 in pioneer days did not sell food or offer beds. Travelers could rent kitchen space to prepare their own food and had to devise their own sleeping space in wagons or elsewhere.

One of Indiana's smallest towns was Gimco City, founded in 1929 on the southwest side of Alexandria (Madison County). Gimco City had nine residents when annexed to Alexandria in 1973.

When the Harbor Hotel opened in 1901 in Indiana Harbor, there were sixty-six registered guests the first night, although there were no beds in the hotel; guests slept in tents or the open air.

The Colgate-Palmolive Company building at Clarksville was once a prison. The state's first prison, established at Jeffersonville in 1821, moved to Clarksville in 1845 and became the Indiana Reformatory for Men in 1891. It moved to Pendleton in 1923. Colgate bought the Clarksville site for $301,101, opening a soap factory there in 1924. The prison initially was leased to private operators, the first of whom was Seymour Westover, who was killed in 1836 at the Alamo.

In 1944 the United States Quartermaster Depot at Jeffersonville provided enough canvas for the military to build a block-wide tent extending from California east to Paris, France. The depot closed in 1957 and became retail shops.

Jackson County, established in 1815, did not have a fixed area until 1859, after eleven shifts of boundaries to help establish neighboring counties.

The Culbertson mansion, one of the most noted homes in New Albany, was an American Legion Post from 1946 to 1964.

Tell City has more streets named for American and European leaders in government, literature, art, and science than any other Indiana town—such names as Mozart, Jefferson, Watt, Schiller, Rubens, and Pestalozzi, a Swiss education reformer.

In research and excavation from 1939 to 1942, about 2.3 million items were uncovered at Evansville's Angel Mounds, which was named not for ethereal creatures of heaven, but for the family that owned the ground before it was bought for the Indiana Historical Society in 1938. It was turned over to the state in 1945.

The site of Francis Joseph Reitz High School in Evansville was once called Coal Mine Hill since it was near John Ingle's Ingleside Mines, established in 1866.

In 1926 the Greater Linton Club sponsored a contest to create a town slogan. The winner, submitted by teenager Otto F. Harding, was "You'll Like Linton," still displayed around the town today.

Jeffersonville was laid out with a checkerboard plan, leaving every other square vacant. The vacant lots were to provide open-air buffers against the spread of disease, an idea suggested by Thomas Jefferson. Increased numbers of land seekers caused the idea to be abandoned in 1817, fifteen years after the town had been laid out.

When a group from Indianapolis went to California and founded Pasadena, they started the town with four thousand acres purchased for $25,000 in 1873. The group went at the urging of Mrs. Thomas B. Elliott because she was discontent with her favorite caladium freezing in 1872. Before creating Pasadena, the Hoosier settlers were known as the San Gabriel Orange Grove Association. Pasadena, chosen at the behest of the post office over the association name, was a Chippewa term meaning "crown of the valley."

The only known war correspondent in World War II memorialized in a monument is William J. Dunn of South Bend. Since he was in a group wading ashore with General Douglas MacArthur on the general's return to the Philippines, the figure of Dunn was included in a memorial unveiled in the Philippines in 1977 showing bronze figures in a wading pool, an attempt to reproduce the scene of MacArthur coming ashore in 1944. Dunn was a correspondent at the time for CBS Radio. Son of a traveling Methodist minister, Dunn lived in West Lebanon, Lafayette, Battle Ground, Otterbein, Medaryville, Greendale, North Liberty, and, finally, South Bend, where he started his journalism career.

Lawrence County was named to honor naval captain James Lawrence, who died aboard his ship, the *Chesapeake*, in 1813 after being wounded in the battle, which was lost to the British. Although defeated, Lawrence gained fame for saying, "Don't give up the ship" before dying.

When the Parke County commissioners settled on Rockville as the county seat, they drank a bottle of whiskey and broke the bottle on a rock as a christening.

Elnora in Daviess County originally was named Owl Town because of the presence of many such birds there, but later was renamed to honor the wife of local merchant William C. Griffith.

François-Marie Bissot, sieur de Vincennes, the French officer in whose honor the town of Vincennes was named, was burned at the stake by Chickasaw Indians in 1736.

National Gypsum's mine at Shoals plunges 515 feet and is the deepest gypsum mine in the United States.

The West Baden Springs Hotel has numbered among its guests Paul Dresser, who composed "On the Banks of the Wabash, Far Away" while staying there, and gangster Al Capone.

Pioneer Mothers' Memorial Forest, eighty acres of virgin timber south of Paoli, was saved from razing by a campaign that raised $24,300 in eighty-nine days to purchase the woods from a lumber and veneer firm.

Nashville originally was named Jacksonburg in honor of President Andrew Jackson; that name lasted only a year.

A spot seven miles south of Paoli is the Indiana Initial Point, established in 1805 by Ebenezer Buckingham Jr. as the point of beginning for all land surveys in Indiana.

Gold mining was begun in Brown County in 1875 in hopes large quantities had been deposited there by the glaciers that formed the hills. Mining was abandoned after no gold lodes were found in fifty years, and the county turned to the gold of tourism.

Parish Grove in Benton County is named to honor Chief Parish, who fell to his death from one of the many tall maple trees once numerous in the area near Earl Park.

Religion

The Bible has been found to contain at least ninety-three names that have been used as names of Indiana communities, including four places named Salem. The state is second in the nation in communities named from the Bible.

Self-proclaimed evangelist Donovan E. Tillman of Indianapolis has passed out millions of copies of a poem he wrote, titled "Life's Stormy Sea," all over the world to people he meets on the street, in airplanes, and in churches. It is part of a promise he made at twenty to bear witness to the Lord.

When the first Episcopal church in Indiana, Saint John's Church, was moved to a new location in downtown Crawfordsville in 1873, the moving rig and the structure became mired in mud in December and stayed stuck until March. Traffic was rerouted for the winter.

The first Protestant group in Indiana was the Baptists, who held services in Knox County in 1798.

Donovan E. Tillman.

Because the First Mennonite Church in Berne once had the world's largest Mennonite congregation, the church structure, built in 1912, was nicknamed the "Big M."

"Bringing in the Sheaves" was written by Reverend Knowles Shaw, who once was pastor of First Christian Church in Edinburgh. He grew up in Milroy, preached his first sermon nearby at the Big Flat Rock Church, and published more than one hundred gospel songs. He died in a Texas train wreck in 1878.

The Spink Hotel, once a gambling casino on Lake Wawasee, later became a religious order's seminary.

When the Reverend Theodore Heck of Saint Meinrad Archabbey monastery turned one hundred years old on January 16, 2001, he became the oldest Benedictine monk in the United States and the second oldest in the world.

Some statuary found at Saint Meinrad was not created when the archabbey church was finished in 1907. Following World War II Herbert Jogerst, a German sculptor, created statues to fill three niches in the archabbey. Jogerst got the job because the chaplain at the Kentucky prison camp where Jogerst was held during World

First Mennonite Church, Berne.

War II was a Saint Meinrad monk. Jogerst's art shop in Germany had been taken over by the French, delaying his return to Europe for three years after the war. During this time he did the sculptures at Saint Meinrad.

The number of students in college plus those in the school of theology at Saint Meinrad in Spencer County once made it one of the largest, if not the largest, such schools in the nation and also one of the largest with a seminary.

John J. Lehmanowski, who served as a colonel in Napoleon's Imperial Guard and escaped a firing squad after the Battle of Waterloo, fled to America and became a Lutheran minister. He had a parish in Knightstown for some twenty years, leaving for Kentucky about 1860.

Francis Silas Chatard, named bishop of the Diocese of Vincennes, was the first bishop in Indiana to have been born in the United States, namely Maryland. The diocese later was moved to Indianapolis.

The First Baptist Church in Hammond has an auditorium that seats 6,400, and it claimed a membership of 60,000 in the 1980s.

When Mother Theodore Guerin, founder of St. Mary-of-the-Woods near Terre Haute, was beatified on October 25, 1998, by Pope John Paul II and canonized by Pope Benedict XVI on October 15, 2006, she was the first citizen from Indiana to be so honored.

Sports

Athletic teams at Shoals were often known as the Jug Rox because of jug rock at the edge of town, a sixty-foot spire with a large flat rock balanced on top. At Spencer the teams were known at one time as the Cops, standing for Center of Population Spencer, which the town once was.

The Hoosier leader in Olympic gold medals is Ray Ewry of Purdue University, with ten golds in track and field. Mark Spitz, who went to college in Indiana, had nine golds in swimming. Ewry was honored with a U.S. postage stamp in the 1990s for his Olympic appearances from 1900 to 1908 with records that included the standing long jump, an event eliminated in 1938.

E. G. Composites Inc. in Indianapolis manufactured bodies for sleds used in the 1988 winter Olympic Games at Calgary, the first bobsleds made in the United States.

The Big Ten was formed on January 11, 1895, when James Smart, president of Purdue University, called a meeting in Chicago of the presidents of seven Midwest universities. They created rules for intercollegiate sports, and the organization, at first called the Intercollegiate Conference of Faculty Representatives, became the Big Ten.

The papers of Rowland P. "Red" Smith, longtime sportswriter for the *New York Herald Tribune*, are held in the Hesburgh Library at the University of Notre Dame in South Bend.

Richard McKinney of Muncie was U.S. indoor archery champion six times, national champion five times, and world champion in 1977.

Barbara J. Hartley of Indianapolis became the first Hoosier woman to ride the Colorado River rapids through the Grand Canyon in an open boat. She was in a party of seventeen, most on rafts, who started the dangerous water sport on July 12, 1985, and completed the 225-mile journey in fourteen days. There are about 160 rapids along the route.

The Clinton Prairie High School girls volleyball team amassed a startling string of 116 straight victories, beginning in 1983 and ending on November 16, 1985, when the girls were defeated by Muncie Burris High School in the state volleyball tournament finals.

For nearly two decades the biggest college program in fishing was at Indiana State University in Terre Haute, where the American Fishing Institute taught thousands how to angle as part of a course for those studying recreation and physical therapy. The course offered one hour of credit and also had noncredit students and involved about fifteen hours of film and lectures on fishing's benefits. The program began about 1973 and ended in the early 1990s.

Baseball

Three of the first four commissioners of baseball had Hoosier connections: Kenesaw Mountain Landis of Logansport was the first commissioner; Ford Frick of Wawaka in Noble County was the third; and William D. Eckert, who grew up in Madison, was the fourth.

In 1943, because of World War II restrictions on travel, major league baseball teams held spring training in Indiana: the Pittsburgh Pirates trained at Muncie; the Detroit Tigers at Evansville; the Cincinnati Reds at Bloomington; and the Chicago Cubs and the Chicago White Sox both at French Lick.

Margaret Gisolo, fourteen years old, was the first girl in history to play organized junior baseball when she played second base for the American Legion Junior baseball team at Blanford, a town south of Terre Haute. The team and Gisolo made headlines by winning the state title, beating a Gary team. They lost their first game in the national part of the tourney. The next year, in 1929, the legion barred

Margaret Gisolo.

THE INDIANA BOOK OF TRIVIA

girls from the program. Gisolo was in the physical education department at Arizona State University until her retirement in 1980.

J. Garland Stahl of Elkhart played first base for the Boston Red Sox in the second game of the 1912 World Series, one of only three series games to end in a tie. The game against the New York Yankees was called at 6–6 in the 11th inning on October 9 because of darkness. Darkness also was why the other tied series games were called in 1907 and 1922.

Lou Criger of Elkhart was catcher in all eight games for Boston in the first World Series in 1903 in which his American League club beat Pittsburgh. He was the favorite behind-the-plate man for pitcher Cy Young, whose name is memorialized in the annual Cy Young Award for pitchers.

One of the rarest of baseball cards is the Gil Hodges card issued in the mid-1950s by the Dormand Company. The exact issue date is unknown, but by 1980 only one of the cards was known to exist. Hodges was from Princeton in Gibson County. He played for the Brooklyn Dodgers in the World Series in 1947, 1949, 1952, 1953, 1955, and 1956, and with Los Angeles in 1959.

Ban Johnson, Kenesaw Mountain Landis, and Ford Frick, all with Hoosier connections, are in the Baseball Hall of Fame, but never played professional ball. Johnson was living in Spencer when he created the American League in 1900; Landis and Frick both were commissioners of baseball.

Amos Rusie of Mooresville was a fireball pitcher who led the league in strikeouts in 1890, 1891, 1893, 1894, and 1895, and is said to have been the motive for moving the pitcher's mound from fifty feet to sixty feet, six inches from home plate.

Mordecai "Three-finger" Brown of Nyesville (Parke County) really had four fingers on his pitching hand, if you include the thumb. He lost one finger in a corn shredder, broke a second finger, and damaged yet another finger when he fell into a rain barrel while chasing a rabbit. A pitcher for the Chicago Cubs, in 1949 he became the first Hoosier inducted into the Baseball Hall of Fame.

Mordecai "Three-Finger" Brown of Nyesville pitched 57 shutouts in his career of 239 wins and 129 losses.

Little is known of the early years of Hall of Famer Edgar Charles "Sam" Rice because a cyclone on April 21, 1912, demolished his home on a farm near Morocco, obliterating family records and killing his parents and his brother and sister. Rice played eighteen years with Washington in the American League.

Edgar Charles "Sam" Rice of Morocco and Edd J. Roush of Oakland City follow each other on the list of all-time three-base hits in major league baseball, Rice with 184 and Roush with 182.

Edd J. Roush, a member of the Baseball Hall of Fame, was a perennial holdout, seldom signing and returning to spring training no sooner than a week or so before opening day.

Edd J. Roush walked out on the Oakland City Walkovers, the first baseball team he played with, because some on the team got five dollars a game and he didn't. His departure caused a furor in Oakland City because he joined a team at Princeton, twelve miles away.

At forty-eight ounces, the bat used by Edd J. Roush was one of the heaviest in baseball.

Edd J. Roush of Oakland City, playing with Cincinnati in 1920, was ejected from a game because he went to sleep in center field while his team argued with the umpire about whether a hit ball was fair or foul in the Polo Grounds in New York against the Giants. Roush didn't awaken when the ump yelled "play ball" after the argument, which prompted the official to oust him.

Max Carey of Terre Haute, a championship base stealer who played with Pittsburgh and Brooklyn in the National League and a member of the Baseball Hall of Fame, was really named Maxmillian Canarius and had studied Latin, Greek, and Hebrew at Concordia College in Fort Wayne while planning to enter the ministry. That goal was supplanted by a career in baseball that began in 1910.

No Hoosier outfielder in major league baseball has more errors in a career than the 235 by Max Carey, who also had a record number of stolen bases, 738, and a record number of assists from the outfield, 339.

Victory Field was preceded by eleven baseball parks in Indianapolis, and seven of them were at one time or another used by professional baseball teams. The first baseball venue was Camp Morton Field near Nineteenth and Delaware streets, used by various teams in 1870.

Don Larsen of Michigan City was only the second major league player to get a most valuable player award in the World Series for his perfect game in 1956. The award was first given in 1955, and the first five recipients were pitchers. In the perfect series game, Larsen threw only ninety-seven pitches, striking out the last batter, a pinch hitter, with five pitches.

Hoosier Donnie Bush made headlines in 1927 as manager of the Pittsburgh Pirates by benching Hazen "Kiki" Cuyler for the entire World Series in a dispute over batting order. Bush put Cuyler as third batter, but Cuyler was superstitious about his usual batting position of second in the lineup and refused to accept the change. Bush said Cuyler could sit out the series unless he agreed to bat third and would say he liked it. Cuyler refused and stayed benched while the Pirates lost the series to the New York Yankees in four games.

Don Mattingly of Evansville is the only Hoosier major league player to hit home runs in eight consecutive games. He also had a record number of grand slams in a season with six in 1987.

When Benjamin Harrison went to a major league baseball game in 1892, it marked the first time a U.S. president had attended a ball game while in office.

Chuck Klein of Indianapolis won the home-run title in 1929 because pitchers on his team walked his opponent for the title five times in the last game of the season. One of the walks was given with the bases loaded. Klein was tied with Mel Ott of the Giants with forty-two homers each when Klein's team, the Phillies, met Ott and the Giants in a doubleheader. Klein homered in the first game, and Ott only got a single. So in the second game Ott was given a walk every time he was at bat, guaranteeing Klein the crown.

Zane Grey played in the outfield in 1896 for the Fort Wayne professional baseball team in the International League, well before Grey started writing the stories of the West that made him a famous author.

The seventeen arc lights that illuminated the nation's first night baseball game in Fort Wayne on June 2, 1883, provided light equal to that of 4,857 gas burners.

Indianapolis is the sole city in the United States to have had baseball teams in the three highest minor leagues—American Association, International, and Pacific Coast—plus early teams in the American and National leagues and the Federal League.

Charles Weeghman, a native of Richmond, bought the Chicago Cubs in 1915, and the team played at a location that later became known as Wrigley Field in honor of the chewing gum magnate who bought the Cubs in the early 1920s.

Major league baseball players Max Carey, a hall-of-famer; Arthur Nehf; Vic Aldridge; Paul "Dizzy" Trout; and Tommy John all were Terre Haute natives, and Mordecai "Three-Finger" Brown, also a hall-of-famer, although born in Parke County, lived and played ball in Terre Haute.

Records of the All-American Girls Professional Baseball League (1943–51), portrayed in the movie *A League of Their Own*, are housed at the Northern Indiana Center for History in South Bend.

Oscar Charleston of Indianapolis, a baseball player often called the black Ty Cobb, hit .353 lifetime in the Negro League, .318 against white major leaguers, and .361 in Cuba, the best of any player there. He hit more than .400 for the season five times.

A game between the Cannelton semipro team and archrival Tell City in 1922 went on for twenty-two innings, lasting four hours and twenty minutes before Cannelton won, 3–2. Buck Altes pitched the entire game for the winners, giving up twelve hits and striking out twenty-one. Chester Leimsruber pitched for Tell City, giving up nine hits and striking out sixteen.

The best average in the college world series by a Hoosier is .714, batted in 1957 by Jim Morris of Notre Dame, who got ten hits in fourteen times at the plate.

Basketball

Newberry in Greene County claims to have built the first gymnasium in Indiana specifically for basketball in 1916. In 1917 the state's highest score in a basketball game up to that time came when Newberry beat Worthington 140–2. Snowden Hert scored ninety points in the game.

When Branch McCracken graduated from Indiana University in 1930 and became coach of the Ball State University basketball team, he was, at age twenty-two, the youngest college basketball coach in the nation. The center on McCracken's first Ball State team was twenty-four years old.

Scott Skiles of Plymouth made thirty assists in a single NBA game, a record, when playing for Orlando against Denver on December 30, 1990.

Of the sixty teams that had won the National College Athletic Association championships through 1999, a total of seventeen were either from Indiana or coached by a Hoosier.

At one time, Paul "Tony" Hinkle, longtime coach at Butler University in Indianapolis, had fifty-five of his former players coaching in Indiana, mostly in basketball.

When playing professional basketball with Indianapolis's Kautsky Grocers, John Wooden once hit 138 straight free throws.

In 1989 Doug E. Curtis, a mathematics teacher at Angola High School, became basketball coach at Prairie Heights High School at Lagrange, about fifteen miles from Angola. He was given approval by the Indiana High School Athletic Association because the Prairie Heights coach left unexpectedly to take a job as principal elsewhere. The IHSAA rules only stated that the coach had to be a full-time faculty member, but evidently not at the same school where he coached.

In the first state basketball tournament sponsored by the Indiana High School Athletic Association in 1912, a total of seventy-seven teams entered; all the games were played on the Indiana University campus in two days.

The first state basketball tournament in 1911 was sponsored by the Indiana University Booster Club; the Indiana High School Athletic Association withheld sanction but did not oppose the tournament. Rochester High School played, although one of its players had attended the University of Notre Dame.

The basketball team at Batesville High School from 1976 through 1979 included six foot, four inch Bill Wanstrath who was born without a left arm. He was the team's tallest member and its best shot blocker. He averaged more than twelve rebounds a game and more than ten points a game, and once came close to a triple double, missing it by only a single rebound. His coaches had praise for his passing ability stemming, in part, from his attempts to hit an open man before being double-teamed. Wanstrath played two seasons at Marian College, played with Indy West in the Indianapolis pro-am league, and became manager of one of his family's five limestone quarries, New Point Stone Company, near Batesville.

Two players from different schools were chosen Mr. Basketball in Indiana for the first time in 1974 when the double honors went to Roy Taylor of Anderson and Steve Collier of Southwestern at Hanover.

When Bobby Plump held the basketball for more than four minutes in the famous conclusion of the Milan-Muncie Central clash in 1954 for the state title, he tossed the ball once in his hands. According to the recollections of one of the game's referees, had he dribbled, it would have been a turnover for double dribbling and would have given the ball to Muncie. But Plump passed the ball to teammate Ray Craft, avoiding the turnover, and got the ball back for his famous last-second winning shot.

The record for outscoring a foe in the Indiana high school basketball tournament was the 156–30 score by Evansville Bosse against Christian High School of Evansville in the 1986 sectional. Previously, Jeffersonville had beaten Henryville 131–78 in 1965.

Ward Lambert, legendary basketball coach at Purdue University, was nicknamed Piggy because of the pigtails braided into his hair as a youth at Deadwood, South Dakota, and at Crawfordsville. Lambert, who coached basketball for thirty years at Purdue University, had trained to be a chemist.

When Elizabeth Dietz arrived at New Alsace High School in Dearborn County to teach English, Latin, and U.S. history in 1927, she found she also was to coach the boys basketball team. She may have been the first woman with such a job in Indiana. The team had a record of 6 and 7.

The Waldron basketball team that reached the Sweet Sixteen in 1927 included twin brothers, Bernard and Leonard Miller, called Ben and Len. Some claimed Waldron, undefeated up to that time, lost to Frankfort 37–31 because the team got to the old Indianapolis Exposition Building, site of the finals, too late to warm up, partly because the driver of the taxi the team took from the hotel didn't know where the building was.

In his first five years in the National Basketball Association, Oscar Robertson of Crispus Attucks High School in Indianapolis, who had been the first black basketball player at the University of Cincinnati before going to the Cincinnati Royals pro team, averaged thirty points, ten rebounds, and eleven assists per game.

The remarkable NBA figures for Oscar Robertson of Indianapolis include 9,508 shots made out of 19,620 taken and 7,694 free throws made out of 9,185 taken. He played 43,886 minutes in his career and scored 26,710 points.

Oscar Robertson and Larry Bird both were named to the five-man all-NBA team nine times, Robertson beginning in 1960–61, when he also was rookie of the year, through the 1968–69 season. Bird was named from the 1979–80 season through the 1987–88 season.

When longtime basketball coach Everett Case, coach of state-championship teams at Frankfort, died in 1966 of cancer, the lifelong bachelor left his estate to his sister Blanche and to fifty-seven former players for him at North Carolina State University.

When all twenty-nine airplane passengers, including the entire University of Evansville men's basketball team, were killed in a plane crash on December 13, 1977, the only person who also would have been on board was Mark Moulton, a broadcaster for the university radio station. Moulton missed the flight because he had the flu.

Oscar Robertson.

Marion Pierce, the high school scoring champion in Indiana for years with 3,010 points until Damon Bailey broke the record, is the sole Hoosier player to have scored more than fifty points in six games; he also scored more than forty points in eleven games. Pierce played one season at Lindsey Wilson Junior College in Kentucky and then quit. In his one college year he averaged thirty-two points a game and scored seventy-nine in one contest.

THE INDIANA BOOK OF TRIVIA

Marion Pierce.

Courtesy of Susan Hanafee

Longtime U.S. representative from Indiana Lee Hamilton won the Trester Award for mental attitude in 1948 as a player for Evansville Central, which lost in the final game of the Indiana state basketball tournament to Lafayette Jefferson, 54–42.

When the Franklin Wonder Five high school basketball team won the first and second of three successive state tournaments in 1920 and 1921, the school had no gymnasium, but used that of Franklin College.

Linda Godby, a six-foot, six-inch player for Warren Central High School, dunked the basketball during practice in 1985–86, becoming the first high school girl known to have done that in Indiana.

The fifty-six points scored by Rick Mount and Billy Keller in the 1969 tournament for Purdue University is a record for a backcourt duo in National Collegiate Athletic Association final four tournament play. Mount scored thirty-six and Keller twenty against North Carolina. But Purdue did not win the tournament, finishing second to UCLA.

The record for most points scored in a National Collegiate Athletic Association tournament game is held by Austin Carr of the University of Notre Dame, with sixty-one against Ohio State in 1970.

The first professional basketball Rookie of the Year Award, presented first for the 1952–53 season, was won by Don Meineke of the Fort Wayne Pistons.

Indiana had four teams in the National Basketball League, a professional circuit started in 1937. The Indianapolis Kautskys, the Whiting Ciesar All-Americans, and the Fort Wayne Pistons were charter members, and the Anderson Duffy Packers joined later.

The Francis P. Naismith Hall of Fame Award for college senior basketball players under six feet tall went to Billy Keller of Purdue University in 1967.

Robert "Fuzzy" Vandivier, star of the legendary Wonder Five of Franklin High School basketball history, got his nickname because one day while playing baseball he was dirty and wearing rough clothing, which made somebody say he looked like "Fuzzy," an unkempt character well known in Franklin.

Wonder Five display, Franklin.

The longest field goal by a female Indiana high school basketball player is seventy-seven feet made by Cheryl Myers of Warsaw, playing for Lakeland Christian Academy on January 20, 1987, in beating Elkhart Baptist, 48–29.

Jerry Harkness, playing with the Indiana Pacers in the American Basketball Association, hit an eighty-eight-foot shot in a game against Dallas in 1967. Pacer Herb Williams, when the team became part of the National Basketball Association, sank a shot of eighty-one feet in 1985 against Sacramento in Market Square Arena.

Ralph Vaughn, chosen in January 1940 as the top basketball player in the nation by the New York City media, was on the University of Southern California team at the time—but he played high school basketball at Frankfort on the 1936 state championship team.

The Franklin Wonder Five won their first game together on November 15, 1918, against Spiceland, 42–6. A week later they beat Broad Ripple of Indianapolis 60–9.

Bobby Fullhart of Muncie vowed to ride nude, strapped to the top of a convertible through the streets, if Muncie Central High School won the state basketball tournament in 1963. The school did, and he did.

In the early days of basketball in Indiana, unusual sites were used. Madison teams played on an ice rink, and spectators could skate before and after the game and at halftime, while Carmel played early games in a lumberyard driveway with lumber piles used as seats, according to basketball historian Herb Schwomeyer.

The Indiana University Boosters Club, which sponsored the first Indiana state basketball tournament in 1911 at Bloomington, invited a team from each of the thirteen congressional districts in the state. The Indianapolis School Board denied participation, so no Indianapolis school entered, leaving twelve teams for the tourney, won by Crawfordsville.

In the 1913 Indiana state basketball finals, the twenty-six points scored by Lebanon's Dick Porter was an individual tourney scoring record that stood for thirty-four years.

When the 1913 Indiana state high school basketball tournament's final game between Wingate and South Bend ended tied at 13–13, it was ruled that the first team to score two points would win. It took five overtime periods of two minutes each for Wingate to win.

In 1918, when twenty sectionals were held to send competitors to Bloomington for the finals of the Indiana high school basketball tournament, Franklin was disqualified because of unsportsmanlike conduct after its victory over Hopewell in the sectional finals.

Doctor James Naismith, originator of basketball, presented the awards at the finals of the 1925 Indiana state basketball tournament.

Burl Friddle became the first person to play on an Indiana state high school basketball tournament champion team (Franklin 1920) and also coach a state championship team (Washington 1930).

When Kokomo reached the final four in the 1941 Indiana state high school basketball tournament it came without squad member Carl "Hump" Campbell. His birthday after the tournament semifinals made him over the age of eligibility.

The final four of the 1969 Indiana state high school basketball tournament included three undefeated teams—Marion, Vincennes, and Indianapolis Washington (the eventual champion)—plus Gary Tolleston, which had lost only one game.

Fort Wayne Northrop had existed for only three years when it became the Indiana state high school basketball tournament champion in 1974.

Bill Harrell, coach of state champion Muncie Central in 1978, also had won the state championship as coach of a basketball team in Shelby County, Kentucky, in 1966, a first in Indiana basketball history.

The all-time individual scoring record in an Indiana high school basketball game is the 113 points made by Herman "Suz" Sayger of Culver High School, which beat first-year high school Winamac 154–10 in March 1913.

Six schools have won the Indiana state high school basketball tournament championship undefeated: Crispus Attucks (31-0), South Bend Central (30-0), Indianapolis Washington (31-0), East Chicago Roosevelt (28-0), East Chicago Washington (29-0), and Marion (29-0).

Swayzee, which holds the Indiana high school basketball tournament overtime record by beating Liberty Center 65–61 in nine overtimes in the 1964 regional, had an enrollment of seventy and had six players on its team.

Coach Ed Denton of Jeffersonville called seventeen time-outs while playing in the 1948 sectional against Henryville. He evidently wanted to reduce the rest time for teams in the second afternoon game. However, New Albany, which won the second game, nevertheless beat Jeffersonville that night, 53–31.

Lowell High School in Lake County lost sixty-two basketball games in a row from 1951 to 1954.

In one of Indiana's major basketball shoot-outs, Ray Pavy of New Castle scored fifty-one points and Jimmy Rayle of Kokomo scored forty-nine points when New Castle won 92–81 in the February 20, 1959, game at New Castle.

After Athens, Texas, won the national basketball invitational championship at Chicago in 1930, a "tour" in Indiana was arranged. Against nine Hoosier high schools, the Athens Hornets won only two games. They beat Brazil and Horace Mann of Gary, losing to Washington, Frankfort, Lafayette Jefferson, Martinsville, New Albany, Evansville Central, and Shelbyville.

Only two Indiana high school basketball players have scored more than two thousand points in their high school careers and also played on a state championship team—George McGinnis of Indianapolis Washington (1969) and Damon Bailey of Bedford North Lawrence (1990).

Cliff Wells coached a Bloomington team on which his brother, Lloyd Wells, played in winning the Indiana state high school basketball championship in 1919; it is the only time in the state tournament history that this has happened.

John Wooden of Martinsville is the only man voted into the Basketball Hall of Fame as both a player and a coach.

John Wooden, although famous for coaching basketball at UCLA, played for Martinsville in the Indiana state high school basketball tournament finals in 1926, 1927, and 1928; was Big Ten scoring champion in 1932 at Purdue University; played professional basketball with the Indianapolis Kautskys; and coached in Indiana at South Bend Central High School and Indiana State College.

Howard Sharpe, longtime basketball coach at Terre Haute Gerstmeyer High School, invented a mechanical man that could jump up and down and wave its arms. Sharpe's aim was to help teach his players to time their shots.

Pete Thorn, a player on the state championship Wingate basketball team in 1914, later earned sixteen athletic letters at Wabash College, a record still unbroken at the college.

Wingate claimed the U.S. championship in basketball in 1920 because it beat Crawfordsville, the only other Indiana entry, for the title in the interscholastic tournament sponsored by the University of Chicago.

In 1914 Wingate won the Indiana high school basketball tournament that included a game against Clinton in which Homer Stonebraker of Wingate scored all seventeen points in the 17–13 victory.

New Castle, a longtime top contender in high school basketball, lost the first game in the school's history, 59–1, against Lebanon in 1901.

In November 1995 Marion Christian School and Union Christian School shot 136 free throws in one game, a national high school record.

The longest goal in Indiana high school basketball tournament play is eighty feet, shot by Gary Matthews of Warren Central High School in a sectional game on February 24, 1971, at Southport at the end of the third quarter. Warren Central beat Marshall, 84–62, in the game.

Although the New Castle High School gymnasium, considered one of the largest in the world, officially seats 9,325, it has held crowds of more than 10,000.

Mike Malone of Lake County refereed his first college basketball game when he was not quite seventeen years old; Hammond Baptist played Fairhaven Christian Academy. Malone had to wait until he was eighteen to be sanctioned as a referee by the Indiana High School Athletic Association.

In the mid-1940s the Valparaiso University basketball squad was billed the World's Tallest Team; several players were six feet, nine inches tall, a rarity in those days.

In 1954, when Milan High School won the Indiana state basketball crown, the town also was celebrating its centennial.

One of the early members of the Harlem Globetrotters basketball team was Opal "Shag" Courtney, a graduate of Roosevelt High School in East Chicago. He played with the team from 1934 to 1936 when the famed touring team had only five players—Courtney, Harry Rusan, Bill Ford, Bill Frazier, and Inman Jackson. Courtney is said to have originated the trick of spinning the ball on one finger.

In what may have been a first in professional basketball, Roger Brown was elected to an at-large seat on the Indianapolis City Council while playing for the ABA Indiana Pacers.

When George McGinnis signed with the ABA Indiana Pacers in 1971 he reportedly got $50,000 a year for three years, a $40,000 bonus, $10,000 to finish college, $20,000 to buy three cars, and a deferment plan to pay him $40,000 for twenty years, starting at age forty-one. It was peanuts to professional basketball salaries and fringe benefits today.

No team in the short-lived American Basketball Association attracted more fans, had more victories, or won more titles than the Indiana Pacers.

The Pacers beat Kentucky 117–95 in the opening game of ABA play in Indianapolis on October 13, 1967, before a crowd of 10,838 plus 1,700 with one dollar standing-room-only tickets. About 2,000 fans were turned away.

After the 1970–71 season, *Sports Illustrated*, in ranking the top professional basketball teams, put NBA teams in the top eight spots, followed by Utah and the Indiana Pacers, both of the ABA, in spots nine and ten.

Talk about players having double doubles in the NBA seldom brings to mind Mel Daniels of the Indiana Pacers, who had fifty-six points and thirty-one rebounds against New York in the 1968–69 season, or George McGinnis, who scored fifty-two points and had thirty-seven rebounds with the Pacers when the team beat Carolina 124–105 on January 12, 1974.

The first person chosen most outstanding player from the final four teams in the National Collegiate Athletic Association basketball tournament was Marv Huffman of Indiana University, honored in 1940. No selection was made in the first year of the tournament, 1939.

Jack A. Hagans of Greenfield, a wheelchair basketball player with the Crossroads Rehabilitation Center Wheelchair Olympians, shot .500 for his career, averaged twenty-seven points a game, and once in his final season in 1972 scored fifty-four points in one game.

Professional basketball's rookie of the year award has gone to these Hoosiers: Don Meineke, Oscar Robertson, Walt Bellamy, Terry Dischinger, and Adrian Dantley.

The first African American player in the NBA made his debut on the court at Fort Wayne on November 1, 1950, when the Boston Celtics played the Fort Wayne Pistons. He was Charles Henry Cooper, who had been drafted April 24, 1950, by the Celtics.

Ann Meyer was the first and only woman to sign with an NBA team, the Indiana Pacers in 1979, but she didn't make the team.

Ann Meyer.

Indiana had two teams in the NBA, Indianapolis and Fort Wayne, from the 1949–50 season through the 1952–53 season. Fort Wayne continued as an NBA team through the 1956–57 season. Fort Wayne won the western division of the ten-team league in 1955 and 1956 and went to the tournament finals in both years, losing to Syracuse in 1955 in seven games and losing to Philadelphia in 1956, also in seven games.

In his NBA career, Larry Bird shot 1,727 three-pointers and made 649.

Scott Skiles, who holds the NBA assist record, was one of the top shooters in the league, with a lifetime average of .890. The lifetime average of Larry Bird was slightly less, .886.

On April 25, 1975, nine boys and one girl played basketball for thirty-five continuous hours in the Dearborn Hotel Gym in Indianapolis to earn donations for the United Way. They scored a total of 19,000 points and raised $300.

Billiards

Harold Worst, a soldier stationed at Camp Atterbury, finished second in the 1951 National Three-Cushion Billiards Tournament in Chicago, having practiced with $50 billiard balls provided to him by famed billiard player Willie Hoppe.

Bowling

Don McCune of Munster won only two bowling tournaments in his first ten years of professional competition, then won six tourneys in his eleventh year, 1973, to tie a record for most wins in a season.

In 1999 three Hoosiers, Mike Aulby and Dick Weber, both of Indianapolis, and Don Johnson of Kokomo were selected among the twenty best bowlers of the twentieth century. The bowlers were picked by *Bowling Magazine* via a vote by thirty-two bowling officials, instructors, and randomly selected members of the American Bowling Congress Hall of Fame.

Dick Weber is the only bowler to win a Professional Bowlers Association title in five straight decades. He won his first of thirty-two championships in 1959 and his fifth in 1992. Weber has bowled in promotions on an airplane, at a rodeo, in two major league baseball stadiums, and on the street outside the New York Stock Exchange.

Diane Bakemeyer, bowling in the 12 to 14-year-old category, scored 736 for a three-game series in February 1985 in the Mike Aulby Youth League at Lynhurst Bowl in Indianapolis. The Decatur Central High School freshman had games of 257, 224, and 255, which was a record in the age category at the time and fourth highest in the nation.

Boxing

The oldest Hoosier to compete in boxing was Ken Snider, a former member of the Indiana General Assembly from Vincennes, who gained a technical knockout over Jerry Strickland in March 1998 in the Pepsi Coliseum in Indianapolis at the age of fifty-two. Strickland, forty, gave up in the second round after suffering a separated right shoulder. Both fighters were about 150 pounds.

The career of Norman Selby of Moscow, Indiana, a successful boxer in the early 1890s under the name Kid McCoy, prompted the expression "the real McCoy." The flamboyant boxer often carried $40,000 with him and was the inspiration for a Broadway play in 1903.

Norman "Kid McCoy" Selby was world welterweight and world middleweight champion in 1900, but life in the fast lane led him to ten marriages and a manslaughter conviction. He was sentenced to forty-eight years in San Quentin Prison on the last day of 1924 for the death of his then-lover, Thelma Mors. She evidently died before she could become the eleventh Mrs. Selby. Paroled in 1932, Selby worked for a time as Henry Ford's gardener and then committed suicide with sleeping pills in 1940.

The former Colemen Restaurant and Hotel at Cedar Lake in Lake County once was known as Russell's Road House and was a training site for such boxing greats of the era as Jack Johnson and Battling Nelson.

Tony Zale, famed boxer from Gary, retired from professional boxing in 1935 after eight bouts. He spent two years rebuilding his body by working in the Calumet area mills and returned to the ring on July 17, 1940, starting a second career that ended in 1949 after eighty-eight professional fights with forty-six knockouts.

The longest, and probably the most futile, boxing bout in Indiana was in Porter County in 1889. Frank Murphy of England and Ike Weir of Belfast met in what was billed as the battle for the featherweight championship of the world. The bout went eighty-five rounds and was declared a draw.

Pat Emerick, who was born in Mishawaka and grew up in South Bend, won the female world boxing championship in 1949 with a technical knockout of Joan Hagen at Council Bluffs, Iowa. Her boxing career started with a loss, but she won seventeen consecutive victories before the title fight. Her career ended a few weeks later when she suffered severe leg injuries in an automobile accident in Michigan City.

Marvin Johnson of Indianapolis was the first person ever to win the light heavyweight championship three times. He won the World Boxing Council title in 1978 with a knockout of Mate Parlov at Marsala, Italy, and lost it in 1970 when he was knocked out in Indianapolis. He won the World Boxing Association title on November 30, 1974, against Victor Galindez in New Orleans and lost it in a 1980 bout in Knoxville, Tennessee. He won it for the third time beating Leslie Steward in Market Square Arena in Indianapolis on February 9, 1985.

Football

Journalist Ernie Pyle, though five feet, eight inches in height and weighing a mere 110 pounds, earned a letter in football at Indiana University as student manager in the fall of 1922.

Floyd J. Mattice of Fulton County was the first person to broadcast a sports event (the 1903 Michigan-Minnesota football game). His description was sent over a special telephone line from the Minnesota stadium to the University of Michigan campus at Ann Arbor, where he was a student.

The Belmont Football Club of Indianapolis, undefeated from 1914 to 1917, had trouble finding opponents after World War I and in October 1922 paid $2,000 for the Oorang Native American team to come to town for a game. The Native Americans, led by Jim Thorpe, beat the Belmonts, 33–0, and also took the best Belmont tackle, a Native American named Charlie "Chief" Johnson, with them when they left town.

Albert Berg, the coach of the first football team at Purdue University, was a deaf-mute who lost his hearing as a youth to a form of spinal meningitis and his voice to self-consciousness about his poor speech. A student at one time at Gallaudet College, he taught for forty-five years at the Indiana School for the Deaf after his coaching debut in 1887 at Purdue.

Cecil Isbell, Purdue University head football coach, called plays from the press box, passing them down to the field via telephone to the headphones of assistant coach Joe Dienhart, who sometimes had the phone torn out of his pocket when somebody on the sidelines tripped over the phone line.

In 1967 Indiana State University at Terre Haute became the first college in the nation to install artificial turf on its outdoor football stadium.

Ernie Pyle birthplace, Dana.

Quarterback Len Dawson, known as the Golden Boy when he played for Purdue University, inspired band director Al Wright to create a Golden Girl as a baton twirler to lead the Purdue band.

George Gipp, the football legend at the University of Notre Dame, went to the South Bend school in 1916 from Laurium, Michigan, in hopes of playing his favorite sport—baseball. It also is said that Gipp once haunted Washington Hall on the Notre Dame campus, after his death, that is.

In 1889 Indianapolis had a Thanksgiving Day football bowl game pitting Purdue University and Butler University for the "state championship"; Butler won 14–0. The crowd was estimated at 250.

DePauw University, which won all seven football games on its schedule in 1933, is said to be the last college or university in the nation to play a football season undefeated and unscored upon. DePauw also was undefeated and unscored upon for the first five games of the 1934 season; Georgetown College scored a touchdown in the sixth game in losing, 49–6.

When Purdue University beat Wabash College 18–4 in 1889, Wabash fans, thinking Purdue had used husky "ringers" from the police force, the campus blacksmith shop, and boiler plant (enrolling them in classes for legitimacy), began calling the Purdue squad names. One name—Boilermakers—stuck and is the Purdue nickname today.

Wabash College defeated Butler University 4–0 on October 25, 1884, at Indianapolis Baseball Park in what is believed to have been the first intercollegiate football game in Indiana.

Wabash College, after winning three straight football games, canceled the rest of the 1910 season when a player, Ralph "Sap" Wilson, died of a head injury in the victory over Saint Louis. Wabash had outscored its opponents, 118–0, before the Wilson mishap and season cancellation.

In 1903 the Wabash-DePauw football game was held up because Wabash included an African American athlete named Sam Gordon and DePauw refused to play. A conference between the DePauw squad and Methodist ministers aided by Wabash graduate Lew Wallace allowed the game to go on. But in 1904 the two teams failed to play a game scheduled for Thanksgiving Day because Wabash had an African American, William Cantrell, on its squad.

There have been seven Heisman Trophy winners from the University of Notre Dame—Tim Brown, 1987; John Huart, 1964; Paul Hornung, 1956; John Lattner, 1953; Leon Hart, 1949; John Lujack, 1947; and Angelo Bertelli, 1943.

Edward C. Robertson of Purdue University kicked seven field goals in one game in 1900, a collegiate record.

The first African American NFL player to start as quarterback was George Taliaferro of Roosevelt High School in East Chicago and Indiana University. He played six years as a professional.

Ralph "Sap" Wilson grave marker, Crawfordsville.

When the future football great Tom Harmon came out for the freshman team at Horace Mann High School in Gary in 1933, he had just won a pair of roller skates in a bubble gum blowing contest. He was ordered off the field for blowing and popping bubbles while the coach was lecturing.

Harry G. Leslie, Indiana governor from 1929 to 1933, served as captain of the Purdue University baseball and football teams in 1903. Leslie was injured in the wreck of the train taking the football team to IU in 1903 for the Old Oaken Bucket game. The crash killed sixteen people.

During the Great Depression, a football game was held between Shortridge and Cathedral high schools in Indianapolis to raise money to help the unemployed. The Thanksgiving Day game raised more than ten thousand dollars.

The Chicago Bears football team conducted their preseason training camp from 1944 to 1974 on the Saint Joseph College campus in Jasper County near Rensselaer.

Mark Clayton of Indianapolis caught eighty-one touchdown passes while with the Miami Dolphins from 1983 to 1992, and seventy-nine of them were thrown by quarterback Dan Marino.

Wilbur Ewbank of Richmond, coach of the Baltimore Colts and the New York Titans (later the Jets), got the nickname Weeb because his kid brother couldn't pronounce Wilbur.

When Bob Griese of Evansville was the highly successful quarterback of the Miami Dolphins, the man regarded as one of the best run blockers in the NFL from 1970 to 1984 was Griese's Dolphin teammate Bob Kuchenberg of Gary.

Andrew Young of Hamilton County helped found, as owner of the Hammond Pros, the American Pro Football League, which became the National Football League two years later in 1922.

In 1966 a total of 745 media members were accredited to occupy the press box when Notre Dame played Michigan State at Michigan State, a record at the time for a single game in an era when press boxes were not noted for their roominess.

When the Indiana Football Hall of Fame was opened in 1973 in Richmond, its quarters were in a former post office, and for some weeks passersby and strangers to town would stop in to get directions to the new post office.

Bob Griese of Evansville Rex Mundi High School and Purdue University was the only professional quarterback to start in three Super Bowls in a row in 1972, 1973, and 1974. He was with the Miami Dolphins. Griese also was the first quarterback to play while wearing glasses.

Marvin Harrison, wide receiver for the Indianapolis Colts, became the first player in NFL history to catch one hundred or more passes for four seasons in a row. He surpassed one hundred catches for the fourth time in the 2002–3 season on November 24, 2002, against Denver. In the three previous seasons he had caught 115, 102, and 109 passes.

Golf

Indianapolis golfer Nancy Fitzgerald won the Women's City Golf Championship in 1976 when she was eight months pregnant. She later gave birth to a son, Andy.

In 1916 Chuck Evans of Indianapolis became the first golfer to win the U.S. Amateur and the U.S. Open titles in the same year.

From July 25 to July 31, 1998, Kent Workman played 1,560 holes of golf, more than twelve holes a day at the Peru golf course, a record at the time. He was a basketball coach at Maconaquah High School at Bunker Hill. His best score for a round during the marathon was eighty-two.

Hockey

In 1972 Niegel Allen of Indianapolis became the only Hoosier and one of three female referees accredited by the Amateur Hockey Association of the United States.

Racing

Automobile

The first official speed of a mile a minute in an automobile on a circular track was established at the Indiana State Fairgrounds in Indianapolis on June 20, 1903, when Barney Oldfield ran a mile lap in fifty-nine and three-fifth seconds during a five-mile heat race. In so doing he broke his own record for a mile on an oval track of one minute and one and two-third seconds.

There were fatalities at the Indianapolis Motor Speedway before there ever was a 500-Mile Race. Driver William Bourgue and Harry Holcomb, his mechanic, died in a crash in a 250-mile race on August 19, 1909. Mechanic Claude Kellum and spectators Omar D. Jolliffe and James West died as the result of a crash near where the spectators were watching a 300-mile race on August 21, 1909. Driver Tommy Kincaid died while testing a stock car on July 6, 1910.

Many drivers participated in the 500-Mile Race starting from the first year in 1911 but are virtual unknowns because they didn't start the race, serving only as relief drivers.

The most rookies in the 500-Mile Race besides the first race in 1911, which had forty rookies, were the nineteen first-time drivers in both 1919 and 1930. There was only one rookie in 1939 and 1979.

Some believe the first 500-Mile Race was won not by Ray Harroun, but by Ralph Mulford, who officially finished second. A mixup was blamed on an unreliable counting system that involved forty race judges each dropping a marble in a tube when an assigned car completed a lap. Mulford thought he had won, thinking his lap was not counted when he slipped through an accident scene midrace. In answer to protests, race officials met the night after the race, reviewed the scoring sheets, and made changes, but Harroun came out the winner. Some who favored Mulford pointed out that Harroun and his car were from Indianapolis, while Mulford was from New Jersey and his car was a Detroit model entered in the race as a promotion. Mulford never pursued his belief he had been robbed, and all records of the race were destroyed after the review.

In 1912 Louis Disbrow drew a spot in the front row (a drawing was held for some early 500-Mile Races) but had to start last because he was late getting to the track. History does not seem to record how late or why, but he was there in time for the start.

In 1919 car numbers were assigned the morning of the 500-Mile Race for fear of bootleg cars being substituted at the last minute.

The Graham automobile, which was the official car of the Indianapolis Motor Speedway in 1932, and the Graham race cars from 1932 to 1935 were from the Graham farm, flour mill, feed mill, and cheese factory in Daviess County.

John Andretti became the first driver to qualify for two races at the Indianapolis Motor Speedway in a single year in 1994 when he made the field for both the 500-Mile Race and the inaugural Brickyard 400.

In 1920 Pete DePaolo was hurt in practice when his car hit the fourth turn wall at the Indianapolis Motor Speedway, so he watched the race from a stretcher in the pits.

In 1923 it was so hot at the Indianapolis Motor Speedway during the 500-Mile Race that only three drivers—Jimmy Murphy, L. L. Corum, and Harry Hartz— drove the entire race without a relief driver.

Pat Vidan, long known worldwide as the flagman for the Indianapolis 500-Mile Race, also was a talented cartoonist who once considered cartooning as a profession.

In 1909 a two-day motor car race was held in Lake County over a 23.6-mile course between Crown Point and Lowell. Drivers made eleven circuits on each day, making the race a total of more than five hundred miles. The event attracted about 765,000 spectators.

Lara Corum and Floyd Davis are both listed as winners of the Indianapolis 500-Mile Race although neither led a single lap of the race. Corum turned his car over to Joe Boyer in 1924 after 101 laps, and Davis was replaced after 72 laps by Mauri Rose in 1941. In both races, cowinners were named since different drivers were at the wheel at the finish.

Wilbur Shaw fractured his skull in a crash in 1923 but came back to win the Indianapolis 500 in 1937, 1939, and 1940.

The oldest driver to officially practice in a car for the Indianapolis 500-Mile Race was Dick Simon, who drove on May 6, 1995, when almost sixty-two. The driver for his car had to be elsewhere for commitments on that date, the opening day of the track that year.

On May 7, 1995, the second day of practice at the Indianapolis Motor Speedway for the 500-Mile Race that year, a lunch break was taken from 2 p.m. to 3 p.m. for the first time in the history of the track. Reaction was mixed, but the lunch time was not repeated.

Murrell Belanger's No. 99 race car, which won the 1951 500-Mile Race, was built on the second floor of a farm implement store Belanger operated in Lowell, a community of about twelve hundred in Lake County.

When cars in the 1909 race from New York to Paris reached Indiana, one Hoosier town exhibited typical Hoosier promotional opportunism by posting a sign reading "Good luck on the Kendallville-to-Paris race."

The infield at the Indianapolis Motor Speedway was once the site of a boat-building operation headed by Gil and Ned Purdy, brought there by Carl Fisher, cofounder of the Speedway, in 1916 from New York. The Purdy Boat Company built boats that were shipped to Fisher in Miami, Florida. Some of the boats contained four hundred-horsepower gasoline engines, valued at $25,000, produced by Allison in Indianapolis. Later the Purdy firm was moved to Miami.

In 1947 four cars were allowed to qualify at the same time on the last day of trials at the Indianapolis Motor Speedway because there had been so many rain delays during qualifications.

In 1988 Bill Vukovich III became the third consecutive member in a family line to drive at the Indianapolis Motor Speedway. He took practice laps in hopes of driving in the race. His father had been a rookie twenty years earlier, and his grandfather had won the race in 1953 and 1954 before dying in a 1955 crash in the race.

A similar scenario occurred at the 500-Mile Race in 2006, when Michael Andretti, whose father Mario won the race in 1969, was in the lineup along with his rookie son, Marco, grandson of Mario. Marco finished second in 2006 and his father finished third. Another son of Mario, Jeff Andretti, also has competed in the 500. Mario, Michael, and Marco took a commemorative lap together at the Speedway to mark the family milestone. The fact that John Andretti, Mario's nephew, also competed at the Speedway marked five members of the family with 500-Mile Race participation.

The jinx against green cars at the Indianapolis Motor Speedway, believed to stem from an early fatal crash in which a green car was involved, was first broken by the Jackson Special. It was driven to second place in the 500-Mile Race in 1946 by Jimmy Jackson, a graduate of Tech High School in Indianapolis, whose school colors included green. After 1947, the last year Jackson drove the car, green remained taboo until Jimmy Clark won the 1963 race in a green car.

The race car operated by Billy DeVore in 1948 and Jackie Holmes in 1949 at the Indianapolis Motor Speedway had six wheels, four in the rear. It also was raced at other tracks. DeVore finished twelfth and Holmes finished twenty-second in the 500-Mile Race.

Paul Russo drove a car with two engines in the 1946 500-Mile Race. It was hard to keep the twin power plants in balance, and Russo crashed in the north turn on the seventeenth lap; Mauri Rose then hit Russo's car.

A. J. Foyt has a commanding lead in the number of 500-Mile Races in which one driver has competed, with thirty-five. His nearest rival, Mario Andretti with twenty-nine, is, like Foyt, no longer an active driver.

Larry Bisceglia was first in line to enter the Indianapolis Motor Speedway track for thirty-seven years when the track opened in preparation for the 500-Mile Race. He died in 1988 after ending his string the previous year.

The first woman to drive the pace car for the 500-Mile Race was model Elaine Irwin Mellencamp, wife of musician John Mellencamp, who piloted an Oldsmobile Bravada to start the race on May 27, 2001.

Kenny Wallace became the first stock-car driver injured in a crash at the Indianapolis Motor Speedway on August 16, 1993, when he hit the pit entranceway during a test run with his Pontiac for a NASCAR race.

In an unusual racing mishap, Howard Hall of Anderson was killed at Funk's Speedway by a race car he had built. Hall was crouched in the pits writing a message to race driver Wayne Alspaugh when the car Hall had built skidded into the pits and struck him.

Janet Guthrie, the first woman to drive in the 500-Mile Race on May 29, 1977, was an aerospace engineer before taking up racing in the 1960s.

A. J. won the one hundred-foot race at the Indianapolis Zoo in 1983 with a time of 13.08 seconds. The Great Tortoise Race was held annually in May beginning in 1981 and coincided not only with the 500-Mile Race month, but also the time when the animals moved from their winter quarters to summer exhibition sites. The speed of A. J. is put into perspective by the slowest time in the first three years of the race, 32.55 seconds by a tortoise that remains unnamed in turtledom. A. J. still was competing in the 2006 tortoise race—against Lyn St. James.

Harness

Daisy Andrews of North Vernon, who in her early eighties became the oldest female harness racing driver in Indiana, didn't start harness racing until she was seventy. She is in the Hall of Fame of the Trotter at Goshen, New York.

Dan Patch, born in Oxford (Benton County), was sold after his first season in Indiana because his owner feared somebody was trying to poison the pacer and thought the horse would be safer out of state. His fear stemmed from the fact that one of Dan Patch's stablemates, Lady Patch, had been poisoned.

Dan Patch never lost a race, but he did lose one of his earliest heats—some said he was slowed to satisfy some bets.

Janet Guthrie with George Bignotti, Indianapolis.

After Dan Patch finished his first season on the Grand Circuit in 1901, blitzing all competition, at least six hundred newspapers published stories telling about his humble Indiana beginnings in Oxford.

Indiana harness racers Rambling Willie and Greyhound both won more money or set more records than the famed Dan Patch.

Red Sails, member of the Harness Racing Hall of Fame and a horse called "one in a million," died in 1954 of tetanus from an errant horseshoe nail after he had been named pacer of the year. He is buried near Crete in Randolph County.

In 1912 a pacer named Single G was bought at Cambridge City's Lackey horse sale facility for $275. The horse earned $120,000 between 1913 and 1927, and in 1950 won the title in a poll as the greatest pacer in the first half of the twentieth century, outpolling the famed Dan Patch.

When Marion Willis Savage, owner of Hoosier pacing great Dan Patch, was told the horse had died on July 11, 1916, Savage himself, already hospitalized, suffered a heart attack and died thirty-two hours later. Horse and owner were buried at the same hour.

Dan Patch, considered one of Indiana's top pacers of all time, was the foal of a mare named Zelica, a Hoosier horse, and Dan Patchen, a pacer from Illinois. In fact, in his first race, Patch was mistakenly listed as Patchen.

The first harness race at the Indiana State Fair, held in 1852 in what is now Military Park in downtown Indianapolis, was won by Copperbottom, who ran the one-furlong distance down a city street. The prize, if any, and the time are not recorded.

When harness racing was a feature of the state fair in 1856, there was a prize of twenty dollars for the trotter that had the fastest mile, but there was a provision that any horse entered had to complete the distance in less than four minutes, a move to keep out draft horses.

The largest crowd up to that time to watch harness racing in Indiana was at the Indiana State Fair in 1905 when Dan Patch was to compete. The crowd numbered at least thirty thousand and some five thousand were standing on the track, which threatened cancellation of the race until they moved off.

Jerry Landess, of Portland, Indiana, was a legend in harness racing, a member of the Indiana Standardbred Hall of Fame (trotters and pacers), and named driver of the year in Indiana nineteen times between 1950 and 1993.

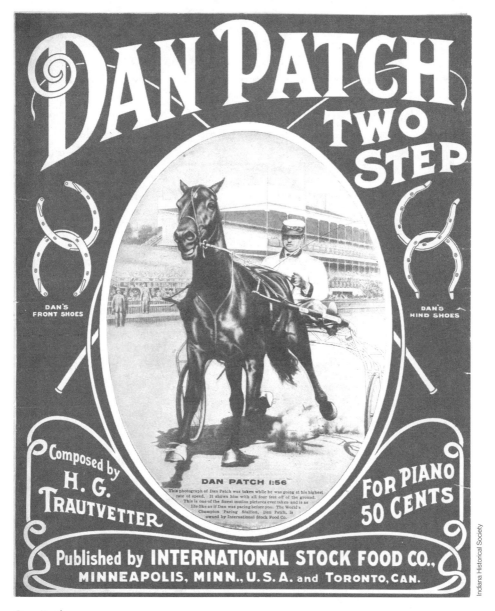

Dan Patch.

Volomite, owned by Thomas D. Taggart of French Lick, was considered the greatest sire of modern harness racing. By 1952 the horse had produced 189 offspring that were racing.

Thoroughbred

The first Indiana-bred horse in the Kentucky Derby was Navajo, who finished seventh in 1973. The first Hoosier-bred winner of the derby was Foolish Pleasure, who won in 1975.

The first pari-mutuel race in Indiana was won on September 1, 1994, at Hoosier Park in Anderson by B. K. Bentley, owned by two Zionsville couples, Penny and Ron Krodel and Nancy and Henry Blackwell.

Softball

Jenny Johnson, a 1968 graduate of Milan High School, is a member of the Slow-Pitch Softball Hall of Fame at Saint Petersburg, Florida, for her play with a Cincinnati team on which she achieved a lifetime batting average of .500. Now Jenny Johnson-Kappes, she has coached girls' softball at Franklin College for many years.

Skiing, Water

Cheryl Riser of Indianapolis won the national title in water skiing in 1965.

When the Indianapolis International Water Ski championships were held on what was called Lake Indy, actually a section of the White River, the paid attendance on August 8, 1985, was 15,123, the largest crowd up to that time to watch water skiing in the United States. The crowd saw Mike Hazelwood of England tie the tour record jump with a distance of 195 feet. Before that date crowds at such events never had exceeded more than 10,000, according to officials.

Swimming

Between 1973 and 1980, the swim team at Munster High School in Lake County, called the Seahorses, won seven boys Indiana state swimming championships; they failed only in 1978 because a flu bug struck the team.

In 1977 Janet Muta of Munster High School became the first female diver in Indiana to win three consecutive state titles and was the first Hoosier diver named an All-American.

Steve Bigelow of Fort Wayne Northrup High School was one of the most successful participants in the White River State Park Games when in August 1985 the freshman won ten gold medals, victorious in all the events he entered, most of them in swimming. They included the 50-meter freestyle, the 400-meter medley, the 100-meter backstroke, and the 400-meter freestyle.

Tennis

In June 1986 Lanae Renschler of Castle High School at Evansville won the Indiana State High School Athletic Association girls state singles title in tennis for the fourth time, a record that can be equaled, but not easily broken. She also finished high school with victories in one hundred tennis matches and without losing a single set in four years of high school competition.

Woodie Sublett of Terre Haute was the first woman named chairman of tennis umpires with her appointment in March 1985 by the United States Tennis Association, which then had been in existence 104 years.

Track And Field

The first Hoosier to receive the Sullivan Award, given to the top athlete annually by the Amateur Athletic Union, was Don Lash in 1938 for his career at Auburn High School and Indiana University, where he set the then-world record for two miles in 1936 during an invitational meet at Princeton. Lash was national cross-country champion a record seven times in a row.

The 100-meter world record of Jesse Owens of 1936 was topped twenty years later by Willie Williams of Gary—10.1 seconds in 1956. Williams ran in the same stadium in Berlin, Germany, in which Owens had set his record.

In May 1985 Arling E. Pitcher of Southport, then eighty-three, set records in five events in the older than eighty age category at the Southwest Regional Masters Track Meet in New Orleans—pole vault, five feet, ten inches; 110-meter dash, 17.16 seconds; low hurdles, 33.14 seconds; high jump, three feet, six inches; and 200-meter dash, 36.28 seconds. Pitcher held more than twenty-five records in track and field for competitors eighty years old or older, including 16.26 seconds for the 100-meter dash; pole vault at 5 feet, 7¾ inches; and 33.14 seconds for the 110-meter dash over 33-inch hurdles.

Arling E. Pitcher.

Science and Medicine

Harold C. Urey, who grew up in Kendallville and won the Nobel Prize in 1934 through discovery of the heavy isotope of hydrogen that made the hydrogen bomb possible, received honorary degrees from twenty-five universities in five countries on three continents. But he passed his final elementary school exam by a single point with a score of seventy-six.

Nobelist Paul Flory, whose work in macromolecules led to the development of plastic, said his interest in science came from his chemistry professor, Doctor Carl W. Holl at Manchester (Indiana) College.

Indiana's first hospital is believed to have been a structure in Vincennes where Doctor Jean Isidore Baty began practicing in 1848. An addition to that building was also used as a hospital until 1865. The addition later was turned into apartments.

A capsule containing viruses, vitamins, insects, bacteria, fungi, and other examples of lower life forms was buried in 1947 in the cornerstone of the University of Notre Dame Laboratory for Germ-free Life. The capsule is to be opened in 2147 for study on the longevity and stability of the specimens.

The first prefrontal lobotomy in Indiana was performed on January 14, 1947, at Methodist Hospital in Indianapolis, although the names of the patient and the doctor were not publicly reported. The woman, who lived in Bloomington, was twenty-five years old and had been diagnosed four years earlier as a schizophrenic and hopelessly insane. She weighed ninety-seven pounds, and twenty shock treatments had been unsuccessful. The surgery, which involves slicing lobes of the brain, took about thirty minutes, and the woman returned home after five days, no longer showing symptoms of schizophrenia, according to doctors.

In 1987 Paul D. Geyman of Madison suffered a life-threatening blood infection (said to result from loss of a spleen sixteen years earlier), and doctors amputated his arms, legs, lips, and part of his nose and tongue in a successful effort to forestall his death.

Investigation of village sites of a people called the Olivers, who lived in southern Indiana from about 1000 AD to 1450, show that they had many tooth cavities, blamed on a carbohydrate diet.

The Canyon Inn at McCormick's Creek State Park, Indiana's first state park, is on land once occupied by a sanitarium built in 1888 by Doctor Frederick Denkewalter for people wanting to "get away from it all."

William Schroeder of Jasper was the second person in the world to receive an artificial heart, but he only lived 620 days with the new heart before dying in 1986.

From the 1920s until 1933 the Indiana State Fair held a Better Baby Contest, sponsored by the State Board of Health's Doctor Ada E. Schweitzer. In 1923 there were nine hundred entrants.

The old pathology building at Central State Hospital in Indianapolis, site of the Indiana Medical History Museum, is the oldest surviving structure in the nation built and used solely for medical education. It was constructed in 1895.

Doctor George F. Dick, a native of Fort Wayne, and his wife Gladys discovered the cause of and a serum for scarlet fever. Dick's test to show susceptibility to the ailment was given to millions of schoolchildren.

The Indiana University Medical School Building in Indianapolis stands on a site where victims of the 1821 flu epidemic were buried—about an eighth of the Indianapolis population at the time.

In 1872 Indianapolis nearly came to a standstill because of an outbreak of flu among horses, the main form of transportation then. The ailment was called gastroerysipelatous disease, or febriguo bronchitis or hipporhinorrhea, experts said.

Brandon Vezeau, born weighing only twelve ounces at Good Samaritan Hospital in Vincennes and later transferred to James Whitcomb Riley Hospital in Indianapolis, is the smallest low-birth weight baby to survive in modern history, doctors said. Brandon, at four years old, was reported to be normal and active.

In 1934 Joe Dienhart of West Lafayette, a two-term mayor of that city and a longtime Indiana football coach, built a telescope 14.25 inches in diameter, at the time the largest in the state.

The first successful Cesarean section in Indiana was conducted on November 6, 1880, in a house along U.S. 52 six miles southeast of Lafayette by Doctor Moses Baker of nearby Stockwell. The mother was Emma Lucas, whose baby, Garfield Arthur Lucas, suffered a scar on the head from the surgery. A Cesarean operation was done in 1827 by Doctor John Lambert Richmond of Indianapolis, but the baby died.

James Taylor of La Porte was the first Hoosier and only the twenty-ninth person in the nation to get polio twice—first in 1940 and again in 1950.

The first DNA bank in the world, aimed at helping families with genetic diseases, was established at the Indiana University Medical Center in Indianapolis in 1985.

The first CAT scan system in the state was installed at Methodist Hospital in Indianapolis in 1974, the ninth system in the United States.

An unnamed Alexandria woman is believed to have been the first in Indiana to bear a child as a surrogate mother, done for an out-of-state couple in 1983.

Mariah Daley of Indianapolis is believed to have been the youngest person to wear contact lenses when she was fitted at twelve days old at the Indiana University Medical Center in Indianapolis on April 22, 1987.

The nation's first lithotripter was installed at Methodist Hospital in Indianapolis in 1984 to use high frequency and acoustic shock waves instead of surgery to treat patients with kidney stones.

A llama from Fort Wayne received a pacemaker in 1987 installed by a seven-man team of veterinarians at Michigan State University in what was believed to have been a llama first.

Eric White of Indianapolis was the first Hoosier to receive a double lung transplant in May 1991 at Methodist Hospital. He died September 5, 1992, of scarring in the lungs.

On January 28, 2002, a veterinarian surgically removed 505 coins that had been swallowed by a ninety-four-pound Rottweiler named Siren of Red Key, owned by Holly Tremaine of New Castle. Veterinarian Jim Wasson said he had found other coins ingested by dogs but never so many and said other vets had removed more money—some finding as much as $140, but never so many coins. The coins swallowed by Siren totaled $23.28 and weighed five pounds. Unfortunately, Siren died of sulfate poisoning.

The first person in the United States to have a successful cervical disk implant was Kevin Wacasey of Brownsburg, who underwent surgery on May 28, 2002, performed by Doctor Rick Sasso, a specialist with the Indiana Spine Group at Saint Vincent Hospital. The implant, which restored Wacasey's mobility in his left arm, was fastened to the vertebrae with two titanium plates. Wacasey suffered the disk injury when an ambulance taking him to the hospital with a heart problem was struck by a cement truck.

About 120 sterilizations were performed in Indiana under a 1907 law that permitted the procedure to curb reproduction by criminals, idiots, rapists, and imbeciles. A sterilization victim's lawsuit overturned the law.

The Gerontology Research Center at the National Institutes of Health in Baltimore was founded in 1941 by Doctor Nathan W. Shock, born Christmas Day 1906 at Lafayette, who devoted his life to the study of aging.

In 1970 Paul Anthony Samuelson, born in Gary in 1915, received the Nobel Prize in economic sciences, only the second time such an award was made. Samuelson was the author of the textbook *Economics*, published in 1948. He was honored for improving the analytical methods used in economic theory.

Former Indiana governor Otis R. Bowen (1973–81) was the first physician named head of the U.S. Department of Health and Human Services. He gained that post on November 7, 1985. Bowen also was the first governor to serve simultaneously as chairman of the National Governors Association, the Republican Governors Association, and the Midwest Governors Association in 1979.

The first time DNA evidence was used in a rape trial in Indiana occurred when FBI agent Robert Coffin testified in Tippecanoe County Superior Court at Lafayette that DNA taken from Danny Flowers of Lafayette matched a sample taken from the twenty-five-year-old rape victim. She claimed Flowers broke into her apartment and raped her in May 1991. Doctor Patrick Conneally, an Indiana University genetics professor, also testified in the trial on November 18, 1992, describing the composition of DNA.

Struther Arnott, Purdue University professor of biological sciences, was made a fellow of the most exclusive scientific society in the world in 1985. He was accepted into the Royal Society of Great Britain, founded in 1662 and admitting only thirty new members a year. Arnott did research on DNA.

Edward Bruce Williamson of Wells County wrote 163 scientific papers while on the University of Michigan faculty. He reportedly had the largest dragonfly collection outside the British Museum.

Things

Several houses displayed at the 1933 Century of Progress in Chicago were later moved across Lake Michigan to Beverly Shores in Porter County. Also moved there was a replica of the Old North Church of Boston, made famous in Paul Revere's ride.

The Indianapolis home of Stoughton Fletcher contained a billiard hall and a bowling alley in the 1870s.

In late 1990 sculptor Harold Vogel of Manassas, Virginia, fixed the nose on the statue of Francis Vigo at Vincennes. The nose had been broken by vandals. The stone used was taken from the same quarry as that used originally for the statue of Vigo, a noted figure at Vincennes for his financial help there in the Revolutionary War. His statue was carved in 1934–36.

Rail line, Crane Naval Weapons Support Center.

When a fifteen-foot chain carved from a single piece of wood was given to President Abraham Lincoln, it was hung in the old state capitol in Springfield, Illinois, where Lincoln met well-wishers after his election. Later when it was discovered that the chain was gone, it was reproduced by Charles F. Morlin of Greensburg, an accomplished carver. The chain replica made in Indiana was hung in the restored old capitol in Springfield in 1969.

The cornerstones of the Indiana Statehouse, built in 1888, each weigh ten tons. This is calculated on the fact that a cubic foot of Oolitic limestone weighs about 150 pounds.

The smallest privately owned electric utility in Indiana was the Greenfield Milk hydroelectric plant in Lagrange County, with eleven farm homes as customers.

The 175 miles of rail line in the Crane Naval Weapons Support Center in southwestern Indiana is the longest military railroad in the United States, perhaps in the world.

The Indiana state flag was designed by Paul Hadley of Mooresville, a teacher at John Herron School of Art, who won one hundred dollars in surpassing two hundred competitors.

A statue of onetime comic strip character Joe Palooka, a boxer, was created in 1948 for Bedford (later it was moved to Oolitic) by stonecutter George W. Hitchcock Sr. He was incensed because in the comic strip the image of Palooka was ordered removed from Mount Rushmore through government pressure. Hitchcock said Joe stood for individualism, self-reliance, and direct action, all of which he considered America's liberties.

The Civil War Soldiers and Sailors Monument in Winchester, at eighty-five feet tall, is surpassed in Indiana only by the Indianapolis Soldiers and Sailors Monument on Monument Circle in Indianapolis. The Winchester monument was built in 1888.

When Interstate I-465, which circles Indianapolis, was built, it was 53.26 miles long on the inside of the traffic lanes and 55.26 miles long on the outside traffic lanes.

Joe Palooka, Oolitic.

THE INDIANA BOOK OF TRIVIA

The first woolen mill west of the Allegheny Mountains was established in Peru in Miami County in the 1800s.

Lake Mead was named in honor of Doctor Elwood Mead of Patriot (Switzerland County), a pioneer in the philosophy of water distribution and a planner of Hoover Dam, which impounded water for Lake Mead. Mead attended Purdue University and became the nation's first professor of irrigation engineering at Colorado Agriculture College. He died in 1936 less than two weeks before the lake was named.

The cattle barn at the Indiana State Fairgrounds is said to be the largest in the world under one roof—4½ acres.

When U.S. 31 was expanded to make it four lanes, the Carter cemetery in Bartholomew County was spared by splitting the road to leave the graveyard in the median.

The Equatorial Sundial in Crown Hill Cemetery in Indianapolis, created by David L. Rodgers in 1987, is the largest of its kind in Indiana.

The eighteen-foot-tall statue *Christ of the Ohio*, which overlooks the river in Perry County, was created by a German artist who was a prisoner of the Americans in World War II. Herbert Jogerst came to Saint Meinrad Seminary after the war to practice his profession of sculpting.

The Indiana State Dental Association, formed in September 1858 in the Indianapolis office of Doctor John F. Johnston, was the first of its kind in the world.

The water clock in the Indianapolis Children's Museum, designed by French artisan and physicist Bernard Gitton, is the world's largest.

A model of Greensburg, built for twelve thousand dollars by the Junior Chamber of Commerce in 1949 for display in Belgium, toured the United States as part of a state department exhibit called America 1950 and hasn't been seen since. At forty-four feet in circumference it was not an insignificant thing to disappear.

Christ of the Ohio, *Perry County.*

THE INDIANA BOOK OF TRIVIA

Fred Cavinder

The famed flowing well at Carmel, noted for its mineral water, was created in 1902 when Joe Carey was drilling for natural gas.

A well drilled on the courthouse square in Lafayette in 1857 produced foul-smelling sulfur water; it was popular for its supposed curative powers, but the supply petered out and the well was capped in 1939.

First National Bank in Richmond, founded in 1863, was Indiana's first chartered national bank. By the 1990s it was also the sixth oldest national bank in the United States.

The cost for illuminating downtown Wabash with electricity in 1880, making it the first municipally lighted city in the world, was $2.50 a night. That was cheaper than gaslights had been.

In the early days of paper plate manufacturing, five of the nine paper plate factories in the country were in Marion. Superior Paperware was the last of the Marion paper plate plants.

The Cincinnati, Bluffton and Chicago Railroad, one of Indiana's shortest lived rail lines, was known as the Corned Beef and Cabbage, a play on its initials.

The Henderson ferry at Evansville, one of two interurban ferries in the United States between 1912 and 1928, was 130 feet long and could carry a two-car train across the Ohio River.

After the merger of three Evansville firms in 1910, the resulting Globe-Bosse-World Furniture Company was said to be the largest in the world.

The most luxurious steamboat ever built was the *J. M. White*, produced in 1878 at the Howard yards at Jeffersonville at a cost of $103,500.

A horse-drawn streetcar started in 1892 between Ewing and Brownstown was the last such conveyance in Indiana when it halted operation in 1916.

A house built in New Albany by William S. Culbertson in 1873 for destitute widows housed thirty widows in its twenty rooms during its heyday.

Florence in Switzerland County once had an anti-swearing society with seventy-five members and a branch in nearby Bethel.

The first Indiana legislature, meeting in 1816, banned puppet shows in Indiana.

An unusual house at Morgantown is made of more than rocks, although rock construction is unusual enough. Hidden in the rocks and mortar and discovered by observers over the years are a boar's skull, pieces of dishes, a knife blade, a doll's leg, a couple of dice, marbles, shells, a much faded picture of the person who built the house (in 1894–96), and the name Isabella. The house was built by James Knight of concrete blocks he made on the spot, impressing stones into the blocks before they had fully dried.

Hoover Dam was built by a Hoosier, Stephan Davison Bechtel of Aurora, whose giant construction firm, Bechtel Corporation, built Hoover Dam, the San Francisco–Oakland Bay Bridge, the first commercial nuclear power plant, and pipelines in Canada, the Yukon, and the Middle East.

Dedication of the *Madonna of the Trails*, a statue honoring pioneer women financed by the DAR and erected on U.S. 40 at Richmond, was performed in 1928 by a Missouri judge who seventeen years later became president of the United States. Harry S Truman was president of the National Old Trails Association at the time of the dedication. The statue is one of twelve across the country on U.S. 40.

A train that operated between Ferdinand and Huntington was sometimes called the Wooden Shoe Local because Ferdinand residents often wore wooden shoes created by a carver who was active well into the twentieth century.

A congressional committee once proposed dividing what is now Indiana into areas that would have been called Assenisipia, Metropotamia, Illinoia, Saratoga, Polypotamis, and Pelisipia. Congress later had second thoughts.

The three-chambered Foote tomb in Bedford, carved from a large stone outcropping in 1840, contains the body of Doctor Winthrop Foote, his medical bag, guns and ammunition in a stone box, the body of his brother Ziba, and Winthrop's horse. Foote, said to have started the first commercial limestone quarry in

Red Cross Farm marker, Lawrence County.

Lawrence County, died in 1856. The body of his brother Ziba was moved from its original burial site on the bank of a pond.

American Mine No. 1 in Knox County became known as Million Ton Mine when 1,062,000 tons of coal were extracted from it in 1926, before the age of mining mechanization. Between eight hundred and nine hundred miners worked at the mine when world production records were set there in 1917, 1921, and 1924.

On old Indiana 37 south of Bedford was a farm of 780 acres that was deeded in 1893 to Clara Barton to become a national headquarters for the Red Cross, which she had founded two years earlier. The land belonged to Doctor Joseph Gardner of Clark County and his wife Enola Lee, an associate of Barton's. Mismanagement and flagging interest by Barton doomed the enterprise; in 1904 the Gardners retook possession of the land. Then their home, which had become a virtual Red Cross museum, burned, ending a dream lost to disillusionment.

Four naval vessels have been named to honor Vincennes: the sloop of war USS *Vincennes*, which sailed around the world in 1829; a heavy cruiser sunk in the

Railroad trestle, Greene County.

Pacific in World War II; a light cruiser that survived World War II and was scrapped; and an Aegis missile cruiser that served in the Persian Gulf in 1988.

At Princeton the first courthouse was the home of Judge William Harrington from 1814 until 1816, when a real courthouse was built.

The Bartholomew County Courthouse, designed by Isaac Hodgson, is said to have been the first fireproof building in Indiana. It was built in 1874 and has been renovated three times.

A limestone slab behind the former house of George Rapp in New Harmony has the imprint of human feet. Their source never has been determined, but some believe they were made by a prehistoric Native American.

The Columbus post office, dedicated in 1970, was designed by an architectural firm in Connecticut, marking the first time privately funded architects designed a U.S. post office.

In the 1930s the Spencer Wood Products Company made millions of clothespins and shipped them all over the United States.

The construction of the highest railroad trestle in Indiana near Bloomfield prompted a rumor that one Italian immigrant laborer (being used in construction) would die every day in building the 157-foot-high structure. But there were no fatal accidents during the dangerous enterprise.

West Boggs Park north of Loogootee is jointly owned by Martin and Daviess counties. It opened in 1972.

The Martin County Courthouse has an element rare in Indiana—a spiral staircase from the clerk's office up to a courtroom. The courthouse in Shoals is the ninth location for the courthouse in fifty years.

A statue of John Owen, victim of appendicitis in 1896, was erected in the Moscow cemetery in Rush County by his parents; disliking the ice and snow of winter chilling the statue, they had Italian carvers make a hat for the statue. The hat disappeared, probably stolen.

An underwater volcanic mountain was designated the Crouch Seamount in 1986 in honor of Purdue University geologist Tom Crouch. The seamount is in the Pacific Ocean between Easter Island and Pitcairn Island.

War and Warriors

Indiana's only naval engagement in the Revolutionary War occurred northeast of Carlisle in March 1779. Men sent by George Rogers Clark seized seven boats and forty men who were bringing supplies down the Wabash River for the British at Fort Vincennes, unaware that Clark and his men controlled the area.

William Tuffs, who was present at the Boston Tea Party and served in several Revolutionary War battles, later moved to Middlebury, Indiana, where he died in 1848. Years after the site of his grave became forgotten, a monument was erected to his memory in Elkhart County.

Jonathan Moore, who served with the Life Guard of General George Washington, the unit whose duty it was to guard the general's headquarters and keep

George Fruits gravestone, Montgomery County.

him safe, is buried in Sharon Cemetery in Bartholomew County. Moore's parents moved to Bartholomew County from Ohio soon after Indiana was opened to settlement.

A minor battle in the Revolutionary War was fought near what is now an entrance to the Indiana Dunes State Park.

One of the few Hoosiers to serve with both the U.S. Army and the Native Americans during pioneer conflicts was William Wells. Seized by the Miami at age fourteen, Wells became a warrior and son-in-law of Chief Little Turtle. Wells fought against Major General Arthur St. Clair in 1791, then switched sides and scouted for Major General Anthony Wayne. Wells died in the Fort Dearborn massacre in 1812. Wells County was named in his honor.

George Fruits, buried in the Stonebraker Cemetery in Montgomery County, is believed to have been the oldest survivor of the Revolutionary War when he died in 1876 at the age of 114 years, 7 months, and 4 days. He had moved to near Alamo, Indiana, in the 1820s and was married to Catherine Stonebraker.

Greendale Cemetery in Aurora is on land once given to Colonel Zebulon Pike in payment for his service in the Revolutionary War. His son, Brigadier General Zebulon Montgomery Pike, discovered Pike's Peak in the West.

No fewer than eight counties in Indiana were named to honor men who fought, were wounded, or died in the Battle of Tippecanoe, which helped send the battle's commander, William Henry Harrison, on to the White House: Joseph Bartholomew (wounded); Joseph Hamilton Davies (killed); Toussaint Dubois; Abraham Owen (killed); Abraham Randolph, (killed); Spier Spencer (killed); Jacob Warrick (died of wounds); and Isaac White (killed). United States losses in the battle outnumbered the losses of the Native Americans, and many historians consider the battle to have been indecisive.

Eight Hoosiers were killed at the Battle of the Little Bighorn, known as Custer's Last Stand, in 1876. They were among twenty-three Indiana men in the Seventh Cavalry, but only twenty-one were in the battle.

John K. Gowdy of Rushville, who served eight and one-half years as consul general to Paris, was instrumental in having the body of John Paul Jones returned to the United States from Paris in 1905 for proper burial at Annapolis.

Only Arlington National Cemetery in Washington has more graves of top-ranked soldiers than Indianapolis's Crown Hill Cemetery, burial spot of eleven Union generals.

At Greensburg an honor walk of memorial bricks was established in 1990 for the more than 330 residents of Decatur County who lost their lives in all the U.S. conflicts since the Civil War.

Edward Black, who was born in Hagerstown in 1853 and grew up in Indianapolis, was the youngest Hoosier to serve in the Civil War. He enlisted in July 1861 at the age of eight and served with the Twenty-first Indiana Infantry Regiment, later the First Heavy Artillery Regiment. He was discharged in 1862 at the age of nine and died in Indianapolis when he was nineteen.

A monument on the courthouse square in Princeton is the only one in Indiana erected to memorialize deceased soldiers while their unit still was active, dedicated July 4, 1865, only three months after the Confederates surrendered. It honors the dead of the Fifty-eighth Regiment Indiana Volunteers and salutes survivors of the unit.

Although Nicholas Biddle of Pottsville, Indiana, was the first Hoosier wounded in the Civil War, his injury didn't come in battle. An African American, Biddle went to Washington with other volunteers to protect the nation's capital. When the volunteers marched through Baltimore, Biddle was struck in the face with a brick.

The cabin in Brookville that was the birthplace of General Pleasant A. Hackleman, the only Indiana general killed in the Civil War, was later moved to Rushville, where Hackleman had practiced law. He suffered fatal wounds in a battle at Corinth, Mississippi.

Captain David C. Van Buskirk of Monroe County was in the Twenty-seventh Indiana Volunteer Infantry Regiment, which was said to have the tallest soldiers in the Union army. When Van Buskirk was captured and sent to Libby Prison in Richmond in 1861, his reputation as "the biggest Yankee in the world" made him such a celebrity that he was put on exhibition in Richmond. At six feet, ten and one-half inches tall, he posed as a freak in exchange for getting all the food he could eat.

Ambrose Bierce, who grew up in Kosciusko County, was wounded in the assault on Kenesaw Mountain in the Civil War; after the war he revisited Indiana once, never to return to the state. He was a noted pundit and satirist and wrote for William Randolph Hearst's *San Francisco Chronicle*.

Colonel Abel D. Streight of Wheeler was captured in the Civil War and helped lead the escape of 109 men from Libby Prison near downtown Richmond, Virginia, via a tunnel from an unguarded and abandoned kitchen. He later was a successful businessman in Indianapolis.

Ambrose Burnside of Liberty, who gave his name to facial hair called sideburns, was governor of Rhode Island for three terms after the Civil War.

Hoosier Lew Wallace was one of the youngest brigadier generals in the Civil War. Wallace was thirty-four years old when the war broke out and gained his rank soon thereafter.

A stately home was built in Greensburg by B. B. Harris, a scout for Morgan's Raiders during the Civil War. According to legend, Harris reached the town two days before the raiders and upon hearing the raiders had been turned east at Vernon, decided to give up scouting and stay in Greensburg.

Henry Dodge, born in Vincennes, led an expedition into the Rocky Mountains as a colonel in the First U.S. Dragoons, marking the first appearance of U.S. cavalrymen in the West.

Willie Cotton of Fayette County was another extremely young Hoosier Civil War veteran. Born on April 17, 1850, he enlisted on July 25, 1861, at the same time his father William enlisted, and became a drummer. Discharged on August 31, 1864, he died of consumption on October 19, 1865.

About 460 Hoosier Civil War veterans, the only men from Indiana on board, died when the side-wheel steamer *Sultana* exploded, burned, and sank on the Mississippi River near Memphis on April 27, 1865. The total toll was nearly 1,600 dead; about 600 survived.

It is unrecorded where Private John J. Williams of Portland, the last Hoosier killed in the Civil War, is buried. It is not known if his body ever was returned to Indiana from Texas, where he was one of the casualties of the Thirty-fourth Indiana Infantry Regiment in a confrontation with Confederate troops after the war supposedly had ended with the surrender of General Robert E. Lee.

Lew Wallace of Brookville and Crawfordsville, after serving in the Civil War, was a member of the court martial that tried those accused of murdering President Abraham Lincoln and was president of the court that convicted and sentenced Henry Wirz, commander of the Confederate prisoner of war facility at Andersonville.

The Greek Revival house in New Bern, North Carolina, used as headquarters by General Ambrose Burnside of Indiana as commander of occupying Union troops in the Civil War, later became the home of C. D. Bradham, who invented Pepsi-Cola.

More than 1,200 Quakers from Indiana, although pacifists, fought in the Civil War in support of their agreement with emancipation. Meetings disowned 148 Indiana Quakers for fighting, and another 220 apologized for going to war and were forgiven and reinstated as Quakers.

When Indiana governor Oliver P. Morton found that Hoosiers were shivering in the Tennessee mountains without suitable clothing, he personally bought overcoats for the troops and sent the bill to Washington, D.C.

An attempt by the military to try and sentence to death three Hoosiers in the Civil War—Doctor William A. Bowles, Stephen Horsey, and Lambdin P. Milligan—resulted in a legal ruling that still stands: the military cannot try civilians as long as a civilian court is available.

General John T. Tilder of Greensburg, wanting the new Spencer repeating rifle for his Civil War troops, borrowed money to buy the weapons and deducted the cost from the pay of men in his Lightning Brigade.

General Jefferson E. Davis, who was at Fort Sumter when it was fired upon and had enough Civil War action to be noted in encyclopedias, was a native of tiny Memphis in Clark County. He fought for the Union and is not known to be related to the Jefferson Davis who was president of the Confederacy. He died in 1879 and is buried in Crown Hill Cemetery in Indianapolis.

John D. Morris, whose home is now the restored Morris-Butler house in Indianapolis, built the home in 1864–65 with money made selling biscuits to the Union army during the Civil War.

Oliver P. Morton, Indiana governor during the Civil War, served ten years in the U.S. Senate beginning in 1867, despite being partly paralyzed by a stroke in 1865.

Winfield T. Durbin, Indiana governor 1901–5, was the youngest of seven brothers who enlisted on the same day to serve in the Civil War. He was fifteen years old at the time and served in two units—the Sixteenth Indiana Volunteer Infantry Regiment and the Thirteenth Indiana Volunteer Infantry.

When John Hunt Morgan and his raiders captured Corydon in July 1863, he charged each of the millers in the town $1,000 to spare their flour mills from being burned. Morgan, finding that one roll of bills he was given added up to $1,200, returned the extra $200.

On July 4, 1866, General Lew Wallace gave the state of Indiana 13 cavalry, 26 battery, and 156 regimental flags from units in the Civil War.

Richard Jordan Gatling, who moved to Indianapolis in 1854, had studied medicine but never practiced as a doctor. Instead, he invented agricultural machinery, which made him wealthy. He also invented the Gatling gun, a new type of machine gun used in the Civil War.

When Hoosier General Ambrose Burnside of Liberty ordered troops into a crater where they were trapped and shot down by Confederate troops, President Abraham Lincoln said, "Only Burnside could have managed such a coup, wringing one last spectacular defeat from the jaws of victory."

New Albany National Cemetery is one of only seven cemeteries in the nation designated by Congress for burial of both Union and Confederate soldiers. It was established by a congressional act in 1862 and is now closed.

During the Civil War the wife and children of Union General William T. Sherman lived in South Bend, where the children attended Saint Mary's Academy and the University of Notre Dame, both of which had junior education programs. In 1865 Sherman attended the Notre Dame commencement exercises. Sherman said he thought being at South Bend would shield his family from the war. The Sherman family lived in the home of Shuyler Colfax, who was in Washington, D.C., as a congressman from Indiana.

Richard Jordan Gatling.

Indiana Historical Society

More than 1,500 African American Hoosiers were among the 186,000 African Americans who served in the Union army during the Civil War.

Although there is doubt that the famed lost order to General Robert E. Lee during the Maryland Campaign could have won the Civil War earlier for the North, there is no question who found the order near Frederick, Maryland, in 1862. It was Private Barton W. Mitchell, who enlisted at Indianapolis and whose family later moved to Bartholomew County. Mitchell is buried at Hartsville, where a plaque about his discovery of the order was put up by the Indiana Civil War Centennial Commission.

The first Civil War monument in Indiana was dedicated on July 21, 1892, at Winchester in Randolph County. Banker James Moorman, a Quaker, bequeathed two thousand dollars for such a memorial and the county appropriated additional money.

Ten men, all Hoosiers or serving in Indiana units and all buck privates, won the Medal of Honor in the Civil War in one day, May 22, 1863, in the battle at Vicksburg, Mississippi.

During the War of 1812 at least twelve Indiana caves provided saltpeter, a main ingredient in making gunpowder, to fight the British, whose navy had cut off foreign sources for saltpeter. Wyandotte Cave in Crawford County was a principal supplier.

American naval officer George Brown of Indianapolis delivered the ship *Stonewall Jackson* to Japan in 1867 and trained the Japanese in its use.

Jesse K. Stork, an Evansville native who grew up in Holland in Dubois County, was the first American killed in the Spanish-American War when his unit was attacked near Santiago, Cuba, on June 28, 1898. Stork is buried at Huntingburg.

When Commodore George Dewey, doing battle against the Spanish in 1898 in Manila Bay said, "You may fire when ready, Gridley," he was speaking to Charles Vernon Gridley of Logansport. Dewey won the fight; Gridley died in Japan, never making it home to Indiana.

Yount's Woolen Mill in Montgomery County supplied cloth to the Union army in the Civil War and to the federal government in the Spanish-American War.

William Conner, who set up a trading post near Noblesville in 1800 and was well versed in Native American affairs, is said to have been the scout for William Henry Harrison and to have identified the body of Tecumseh at the pivotal Battle of the Thames in 1813.

During World War I, anti-German feelings ran high in Indianapolis, causing the city to change the name of Germania Street to Belleview Place and Bismarck to Pershing Avenue.

Marshal Foch of France, considered by some to be the greatest general of World War I, visited Indiana on November 4, 1921.

Brace Beemer of Vincennes was the youngest sergeant in the army in World War I because he lied about his age and enlisted at fourteen. He later was the third person to provide the voice of the Lone Ranger on radio.

Alice Dodd of Evansville was the first Hoosier to get a World War I pension by virtue of her son, James B. Gresham, being one of three soldiers who were the first Americans killed in the war. Dodd also was honored with a home built by public donations at Evansville.

Henry Thornton, who lived as a youth in Logansport, administered Britain's railroads during World War I and was knighted for his efforts by King George V.

Howard Boegaholtz of Johnson County was one of six men chosen to accompany the body of the Unknown Soldier from France to the United States in November 1921 to establish the national memorial in Arlington National Cemetery.

A grove of Norway maples was planted at Aurora in 1919 to honor servicemen who died in World War I. In 1921 trees were planted there for men who enlisted in that war, and in the same year 330 trees were planted in Garfield Park in Indianapolis in honor of Marion County casualties in the war.

The Indiana World War Memorial in Indianapolis is patterned after the mausoleum created as a tomb for King Mausolus by Queen Artemisia in 350 BC at Halicarnassus, Turkey.

Brigadier General Anson Mills, a native of Thorntown, designed the woven cartridge belt used by the army for years.

The first attack on the Japanese homeland in World War II, carried out on July 14, 1945, by the Pacific fleet, included the battleship *Indiana*. Ironworks in the coastal city of Kamaishi, Honshu, were damaged.

The first of nineteen prisoners of war to die at Indiana's Camp Atterbury near Edinburgh in World War II was Francisco Tota of Italy, whose death was on February 28, 1944.

Alexandria was featured in a booklet *Small Town USA*, issued in 1944 through the Office of War Information to correct foreign ideas in World War II about typical Americans.

American War Mothers was organized in 1918 by Alice Moore French of Trafalgar at the suggestion of noted Hoosier writer and humorist Don Herold. Originally started to promote conservation of food during World War I, the group's aim of supporting those in the military and their families has been expanded and the organization renewed war-by-war ever since. French was the organization's first national president.

Stout Field in Indianapolis was a World War II base for training pilots for troop transports and gliders.

Freeman Field at Seymour had these remarkable functions in World War II: captured enemy aircraft were taken there to be tested and some parts were buried there after the war when the field became a civilian airport; the last military fatality there, Lieutenant William V. Haynes, died in the crash of a captured German fighter; in 1944 the field was designated the first helicopter training base in the nation; a refusal in 1945 to admit African Americans to the officers' club created a national story when three African Americans were arrested for insisting on admission to the club. The incident was said to have played a major role in desegregation of the armed forces in 1949 by order of President Harry S Truman.

Construction of Camp Atterbury in the spring of 1942 brought so many workers to Edinburgh, swelling the population from 2,466 to more than 4,000 in only four months, that even rooms at the funeral home were rented to live people.

Creation of Camp Atterbury during World War II displaced the small towns of Kansas and Pisgah.

Camp Atterbury was named to honor the little-known Brigadier General William Wallace Atterbury of World War I, who was born in New Albany in 1886.

In March 1922 Schoen Field was dedicated at Fort Benjamin Harrison in Indianapolis, a site used by mail planes and to train Indiana National Guardsmen. The airfield continued in use until late 1945 when it was deactivated. It made a short revival from 1947 to 1950, but all traces are gone now.

Lieutenant Raymond E. Hine of Indianapolis perished at the controls of a P-38 Lightning plane in an attack in April 1943 that killed Japanese Admiral Isorokue Yamamoto, the man who planned the attack on Pearl Harbor. The attack at Bougainville in which Hine died was kept secret for two years.

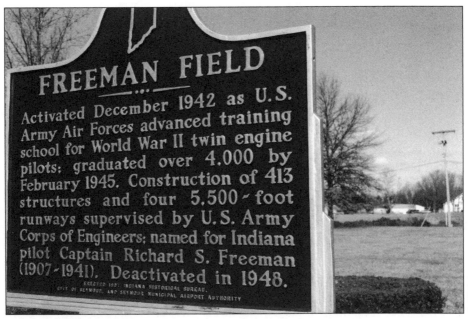

Freeman Field, Seymour.

Because of her campaign to line U.S. 41 with flags to honor men in uniform, Mary Lou Kieswetter was designated Indiana's Flag Lady by the 1969 Indiana General Assembly. She was a resident of Highland in Lake County when she spearheaded a flag memorial to servicemen and later moved to Valparaiso.

Italian-born Vincent A. Lapenta, who came to Indianapolis in 1911 and gained fame as a surgeon at Saint Francis Hospital, was named Italian consular agent to Indiana in 1921, but in 1941 was held at Fort Benjamin Harrison as an enemy alien when Italy declared war on the United States.

Leslie Johnson of Indianapolis organized the first reunion of Navy Patrol Craft veterans in 1987 and became first president of the Patrol Craft Sailors Association. Patrol Craft were used in World War II to protect merchant ships.

The Link Trainer, used by the military to teach hundreds how to fly, was invented by Edwin Link, born in Huntington, when he was twenty-four years old. The device earned him the nickname "the pilot maker."

The World War II buzz bomb long displayed on the courthouse lawn at Greencastle was obtained from the U.S. Army Ordnance Division in Maryland in 1946, only two years after the first buzz bomb landed on a London suburb.

Lieutenant General Walter Bedell Smith of Indianapolis, who signed the armistice in September 1943 ending World War II hostilities with Italy and the 1945 document at Reims, France, in which Germany surrendered, began military life as a private in the Indiana National Guard.

During World War II 160 landing ship tanks (LSTs) were built at Evansville and sailed to the ocean via the Ohio and Mississippi rivers. The first LST was launched on October 31, 1942, only 234 days after a newly organized company signed a contract to build the vessels.

When Lucille Pryor Fultz of Indianapolis was in the navy in World War II, she was stationed in Washington, D.C., and became the first woman in military uniform to be admitted to practice before the U.S Supreme Court. In Washington she was part of the tax section of the Judge Advocate General of the navy.

The Finance Center at Fort Benjamin Harrison in Indianapolis, built in 1953 and later renamed the Major General Emmett J. Bean Center, is an army property second in size only to the Pentagon.

In 1992 the U.S. Navy bought all of Glendora Lake in Sullivan County from Amax Coal Company, using the mile-long, one hundred-foot deep body of water for testing underwater listening devices. It was the only lake fully owned and operated by the navy.

Richard Eugene Millis of rural Henry County was the first Indiana casualty in the Korean War, killed on June 10, 1950, in a plane crash near the Korean War front five days after that war started. He was buried in Greensboro. He also had served in the army in World War II, having been drafted in 1944 and sent to the Philippines.

Gene Eckerty of Gibson County was the only sitting member of the Indiana General Assembly to be killed in World War II. He was reelected to the Indiana House of Representatives in 1944 although he had been drafted in August 1943. He was killed in Germany on February 25, 1945, and was buried in Princeton.

James Robert Sordelet of Fort Wayne reenlisted in the navy on August 3, 1958. At the time he was aboard the submarine *Nautilus*, which was under the North Pole, marking the first time anyone has reenlisted in that situation.

Army Private Michael Hoey, age twenty-four, serving in Saudi Arabia in 1991, randomly picked a letter addressed to "any soldier" and found it was from his sixteen-year-old sister Jennifer Hoey, half a world away in Richmond, Indiana. Schoolchildren sent thousands of letters to "any soldier" to boost troop morale.

A book, *The Man That Went Away*, was sent in 1943 to Allen Shively of Mount Summit, who was in the army on Guadalcanal, but never reached him. The book was found by his niece, Debby Shively, on eBay, who purchased it and gave it to Allen on Christmas in 2001, fifty-eight years after it had been sent and never received.

The first city ceremony to give a special thanks to veterans of the Vietnam War was held in Indianapolis in April 1985. It was organized by Loc To, a Vietnamese who was an analyst at Eli Lilly and Company.

Index